Unforgettable

GOD'S RELENTLESS HEART
FOR HIS DAUGHTERS

STEPHANIE G. HENDERSON

CROSSBOOKS'
PUBLISHING

CrossBooks™
A Division of LifeWay
1663 Liberty Drive
Bloomington, IN 47403
www.crossbooks.com
Phone: 1-866-879-0502

Scripture taken from the New King James Version except where indicated. Copyright 1979, 1980, 1982 by Thomas Nelson, inc. Used by permission. All rights reserved.

First published by CrossBooks 10/22/2012

ISBN: 978-1-4627-2127-6 (sc)
ISBN: 978-1-4627-2125-2 (hc)
ISBN: 978-1-4627-2126-9 (e)

Library of Congress Control Number: 2012917327

Printed in the United States of America

This book is printed on acid-free paper.

I could never forget you ...
I've carved your name on the palm of my hand
Isaiah 49: 15b–16a (NIV)

Stephanie G. Henderson

Foreword by Pam Boyd

CONTENTS

About Pam Boyd

Pam Boyd is a personal friend and mentor, and she serves as the women's pastor at New Life Church in Colorado Springs, Colorado. She serves her family and leads the church with an Audrey Hepburn–type grace and a quiet strength, which is so admirable and beautiful. Loving her family is her first priority, and this love is obvious in the way she exemplifies balancing her busy life with a deep affection for Brady, Abram, and Callie.

I told Pam several months ago that I needed to be obedient to the Lord and write this book. She was such an encouragement and cheerleader for this project; however, I continued to say, "I need to write this book" without actually sitting down and doing it.

We completed our spring conference and were enjoying dinner together with our leadership team to celebrate its success. Lynette Lewis, founder of Stop Child Trafficking Now, speaker, and author, talked about her success in writing and shared some wisdom on the topic. She said, "You cannot allow the hesitations to become stop signs where you park your car and remain." That thought impacted me. One of the main reasons the book was still in my mind and not on paper was because I had many hesitations in the process.

Pam turned to me and asked, "When are you going to write your book?" I looked at her, smiled, and said, "I guess I'm parked at the stop signs!" We laughed. Pam then offered encouragement and said, "It's time to move past the stop signs, Steph!" She was right, and I needed that affirmation and push from the ledge where I had remained for months.

Thank you, Pam, first for being such a precious friend and for being a bold, godly woman who gave a word regarding my hesitations at the right time. Thanks for pushing me from the ledge. You are a treasure in my life.

> Like apples of gold in settings of silver is a word spoken in right circumstances.

> Proverbs 25:11(NIV)

FOREWORD

By Pam Boyd

Can you even begin to imagine yourself as "unforgettable"? To our dear loved ones, we can imagine an inkling of being unforgettable, right? But to our God, we cannot begin to fathom it.

Ephesians 1:11–12 (MSG) sums up just how God sees us as unforgettable. In the verse, Paul writes, "It's in Christ that we find out who we are and what we are living for. Long before we first heard of Christ and got our hopes up, he had his eye on us, had designs on us for glorious living, part of the overall purpose he is working out in everything and everyone."

Daughters, our God said He had plans for us for a "glorious" living long before we even first heard of Him! We were unforgettable before we even knew Him. That, my friends, astounds me. I am in constant awe of just how much He really does love me and continues to love me no matter how much I mess up. His love for me is an ocean of grace, and it is for you, too.

In this book, Stephanie invites you to become a passionate, bold, God-fearing daughter of God. Her inspiring stories from her childhood throughout her adulthood give us all hope that although we may not have always behaved like His daughter, it is not too late to start behaving like one through simple obedience in His guidance and understanding of His great love.

Your confidence in who you are in God flourishes in His guidance and love. You begin to see yourself as God sees you—an unforgettable daughter in the King of kings.

This concept took many years for me to wrap my head around. I grew up a very quiet, shy little girl who became a very quiet, shy young lady. I didn't have a personal relationship with God until my late teens. In my childhood, I knew about God and that I loved Him; but not until I was eighteen did we become friends—a friend who desires me to talk to Him and share all of me with Him, including my feelings; my hurts and struggles; and my dreams, hopes, and desires.

I was thirty-eight years old when I truly accepted how and why God made me the way I am. I always had questioned why He made me quiet and not outspoken like most of my friends. He showed me in His word the reason; from then on I have never once regretted my quietness. After asking God what it was that He wanted me to see on my personal heart quest with Him, he led me to 1 Peter 3:1–4 (NIV)that says "And let not your adornment be merely external … but let it be the hidden person of the heart, with the imperishable quality of a gentle and quiet spirit, which is precious in the sight of God." Daughters, I encourage you to receive that verse in your heart as confirmation that God truly does love you just the way you are.

Living and behaving as a daughter of God takes a lot of faith and courage. At times we will walk through the valley with heartaches and pain. I love how Stephanie shows us in this book how the valley doesn't have to be our final resting place. We must believe in His faithfulness to see us through the valley more than we are overwhelmed by our circumstances. God's word is true. He will never leave us or forsake us. What an incredible promise He has made us!

Daughters, God does not make mistakes. He created you in His image. He knew you before you were formed in your mother's womb. His love for you spreads as far as from the east to the west.

You are in the palm of His hand. When you begin to see yourself as God sees you, you really are unforgettable.

Let's grab hold of this endearing title as daughters of God, and let's be carriers of His presence as His daughters to a hurting and lonely world full of unforgettable daughters.

ACKNOWLEDGMENTS

This book is dedicated to several important people in my life. First and foremost, I could not have ever had my dreams realized without my husband, George, and his influence in my life. His constant belief in me, even when I wasn't sure I believed in myself, has given me the courage to take steps much larger than ever I imagined. He is the steady hand, strong voice of wisdom, and loving arms that hold me. Thank you, honey, for always seeing God's potential for me and not allowing me to settle. Thank you for loving me and loving the dream within me.

Secondly, I dedicate this book to my father, Bill Spooner. He has exemplified a godly, gentle heart accompanied with a strong belief in God's goodness. Being the only daughter in our family, I am his "favorite" daughter. Thank you, Dad, for giving me a lifetime of memories and teaching me the unconditional love of Jesus through your life. It has made embracing God as my Father an easier step because of your example.

I thank my three children, Jessica, John Mark, and James. Watching their relationships mature with the Lord has been the best gift. They inspire me, make me laugh until it hurts, and have been faithful in saying, "You can do it, Mom." Thank you so much for your love and support. I am so blessed to be your mom.

I am most thankful to my heavenly Father, Jesus Christ. Through times in the valley, the foxholes, and the mountain tops, He has remained faithful. I'm so thankful for the hard times where truly He became my portion and my Father. I am amazed at the grace, strength, and mercy available to me every day. I am so proud to be His daughter.

1

THE DAUGHTERHOOD REVELATION

UNFORGETTABLE

THE DAUGHTERHOOD
Revelation

Peace …does not mean to be in a place where there is
not noise, trouble, or hard work. It means to be in the
midst of those things and still be calm in your heart.

—Unknown

I was in the Denver International Airport waiting for my
flight to depart. I was headed to Florida to conduct a women's
conference. As I patiently sat waiting for my plane to begin boarding,
repeated announcements caught my attention. As I listened more
closely, I realized the announcements all had one thing in common:
flight delays. Denver can commonly get wind gusts and random
snowstorms, even in the middle of May. I began to more closely
monitor my own flight in case the delays would affect me, because
I was on a tight schedule for this particular weekend conference. I
typically would fly out a day prior to the conference beginning in
order to have necessary meetings and to prepare for the weekend.
However, this time I chose to fly on the day that my leadership
commitments began. I had a leadership meeting scheduled almost
immediately upon my arrival in Tampa.

As I continued to watch the announcements, I noticed the flight status board change. Within a few moments, I then heard the gate agent say, "Attention airline customers scheduled on Flight 1062 to Tampa, Florida. Your flight has been delayed due to inclement weather we are experiencing. We will update you as soon as we have information regarding your flight." I sat back in my chair and sighed with frustration. What was I going to do if my flight was delayed for several hours? I needed to be in Tampa on time in order to conduct the leadership meeting I had planned.

My mind started racing with the various scenarios should my flight be delayed much longer. I could feel the anxiety begin to rise as I pondered all the consequences of not arriving on time. I decided to pray.

I started walking around the terminal and talking to the Lord (in my heart, of course). I said, "Father, this flight is late and I might miss my meeting. The ladies are waiting on me, and this is our only chance to meet before the conference begins. I need to be on that flight!" While hoping the status would change, I thought, *Maybe there's another flight I could take?*

I walked to the counter and stood in line with at least fifteen other people who all seemed to be waiting to ask the same question. I overheard the gate agent's responses to the people in front of me. It looked grim, but I remained in line focused on trying my best to get on another flight.

I finally approached the desk and asked if another flight to Tampa was available. The gate agent said, "Well, there is another flight, but it's completely booked. I can try and put you on standby if you'd like." I thanked the gate agent for her help and explained that I was facilitating a meeting, and it was really important that I arrive on time. The gate agent courteously listened, shook her head, and called the next in line. I returned to walking and praying.

Now that I knew that the next flight was already overbooked, I became quite concerned. I again began to pray and said, "Father, do you know that the next flight is overbooked and my flight is delayed? I'm on standby, but they are not really concerned about me missing the meetings." The Lord was quiet.

As I stood in the terminal waiting for God to answer, I began a personal survey of any unconfessed sin that might be lingering, thus keeping me from getting on a flight. I thought through my morning and conversations with my family to check whether I was harboring sin of any sort. I did get frustrated when my luggage rolled around the parking lot while I was trying to get in the shuttle bus. There was that person sitting next to me that really annoyed me by talking too loudly on her cell phone. There's also a strange smell in the terminal, and I guess I've tried to figure out who hasn't bathed lately. As I pondered these things in my heart, I said, "Father, please forgive me. I'm sorry for my impatience and for judging the bad-smelling passenger. Amen." I thought that as soon as I said "Amen," the plane would magically arrive. It did not.

I then thought that maybe I should do something sacrificial in order to prompt God's favor with my plane arrival. I had rushed out of the house in order to get to the airport on time without coffee. Now *that* is sacrificial! Furthermore, I thought that I would forego the latte that I was really looking forward to enjoying. Okay, I thought, "Now I'm fasting. I'm praying, I'm caffeine-deprived, and I've confessed my sin of impatience and bad-smelling passenger judgment, so where's the plane?" No plane arrived, and all I heard from God was radio silence.

At this point, I was really getting uncomfortable with the situation. My impatience grew and I started developing a headache, which was probably caused by my extreme fasting and my extreme caffeine deprivation. I continued to walk and pray, and I said to the Lord, "Now Father, you do realize that this is not a vacation. It is very sacrificial because, after all, you know how much I love the

4

beach and I will not even enjoy it for one moment! I mean, I'm going to *work* and work for you, by the way. You've called me to do this, I'm being obedient, I'm … I'm … I'm sacrificing my time for what you've called me to do, and all I'm asking is that you miraculously provide a plane." The Lord was still silent. My headache was growing along with my impatience for what, in my opinion, could have been quickly resolved by God's intervention.

My earnest prayer continued, "Lord, what am I going to do? What if I don't make it to Tampa? What if I don't even arrive by the next day and miss the conference all together? They've planned, marketed, and worked so hard for this to be successful. What will happen?" I finally said, "Lord, what do you have to say about all of this?" I stopped walking and stood still, waiting for an answer to my obviously urgent request. Again, just silence.

I've known the Lord since I was eight years old. I also know from experience that when God is silent, it's usually because I'm not ready for the answer or I'm not ready to listen. He waits to have my complete attention, so I found a quiet place to sit, placed my baggage by my feet, and just waited. After a few moments, I said, "Okay, I'm ready to listen. What, Father, are you going to do?"

After a few moments, the Lord spoke to my heart, and said, "You need to stop it." That was it. I thought, *What? What does that mean?*

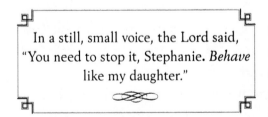

In a still, small voice, the Lord said, "You need to stop it, Stephanie. *Behave* like my daughter."

I was stunned at this response. Like a load of bricks on my head, I realized that God was teaching me something that had nothing to do with delayed or cancelled flights. As I pondered the statement, "*Behave* like my daughter," I realized that I had no idea how to do what he said or what that fully meant. I sat in silence. I finally said, "Father, I have no idea how to do that." I remained quiet for several minutes to really take this phrase in. How does a daughter *behave?* I asked the Lord for wisdom to know what I should say next because I honestly had no clue.

After several more minutes of searching God's heart for wisdom, I said, "Father, you know what I need. Your Word says, "Your Father knows what you need before you ask him" Matthew 6:8b (NIV). You already understand the importance of this weekend, and I'm going to wait and trust that you will make a way." As the words of my prayer were whispered from my heart, I felt this overwhelming sense of peace surround me. I also realized that my Father is able to handle this situation, and my need is already urgent in his hands.

A few minutes later, an announcement came from the flight desk, "Stephanie Henderson, would you approach the flight desk, please?" I walked up, and to my surprise, the gate agent handed me the *last* ticket for the *last* seat on the oversold flight. I arrived fifteen minutes late to Tampa, but right on time for my meeting.

This experience challenged my understanding of daughterhood. Even though I have known the Lord as my Savior since childhood, what God revealed to me in the Denver airport was different in many ways. Although I have known Him all these years, I never fully comprehended how to respond to Him as a daughter. I was curious about this new depth of understanding and aware that there was something so much more in my relationship with Christ that had been missing. I honestly had no idea what it was, but I knew God was leading me on a journey to discover the answer.

Upon returning home from the conference in Florida, I began researching Scriptures on the concept of being God's daughter. As I studied God's Word and spent time seeking God's heart for me, His daughter, I realized that within the years of serving God, a degree of intimacy and trust was missing. Through this discovery, the Lord has taught me the beautiful truth of behaving like his girl. This understanding of the Father's heart has brought a level of peace, confidence, and security that I had not yet known.

I looked back on my life at the many times I felt like maybe God had forgotten me. Sometimes I needed to wait for an answer, and I had mistakenly believed that His promises were for others and not for me. I've faced disappointments and challenges in which I had difficulty seeing God's hand in my life. At other times I felt so alone and wondered if God even knew. This depth of understanding of daughterhood challenged those times as I looked back over the years.

As Isaiah 49:15b–16a (NIV) says, "I could never forget you … See, I have even engraved your name upon the palm of my hand." This verse speaks volumes to those times when I misunderstood my value to my heavenly Father. My name is engraved on the palm of His hand — a promise of His covenant in our relationship.

> As Isaiah 49:15b–16a (NIV) says, "I could never forget you … See, I have even engraved your name upon the palm of my hand."

Through these next several chapters, we will peer into the life of Hannah, who exemplified persistence in prayer; into the courageous heart of Jochebed, the mother of Moses; into the favored stance of Elizabeth, the mother of John the Baptist; and Mary, the mother of Jesus; and into the expression of forgiveness of the adulterous woman, Mary Magdalene. We will discover the life-transforming truths of daughterhood as portrayed in these powerful women's lives.

My wish is for you to be able to reframe the way you think about yourself and the way God views you. God is relentless in His pursuit of having relationship with you, bringing peace and healing in your life, and showing you how to live a life victoriously. He wants to unfold His amazing destiny He has planned.

As children of God, we are not numbered placeholders in a sea of humanity. We are His. We are His one and only, as far as He is concerned. We matter.

My prayer is that this teaching will impact your life as much as it has impacted mine. My hope is that you also will realize that as a daughter of the living God, you too are truly unforgettable.

2

EMBRACING DAUGHTERHOOD 101

Unforgettable

Embracing
Daughterhood 101

They will be able to say that when she stood in the
storm ... and when the wind did not blow her away, and
it surely has not, she adjusted her sails.

—Elizabeth Edwards

December 21, 2009, was an ordinary day with ordinary
happenings—waking up, sipping coffee, doing chores, and
feeling rather content in the everyday routine of life. We were
preparing for the upcoming Christmas holidays with menu planning,
gift buying, and my never-ending need to tweak my holiday
decorations just once more.

Our family gatherings often revolve around food. Planning,
preparing, and cooking the food together are part of the way we bond
as a family. We like to prepare both nontraditional items and comfort
holiday foods that bring about sweet memories. We plan appetizers,
salads, main courses, and, of course, desserts. I enjoy decorating for
the holidays and making sure the table is elegant, beautiful, and filled
with lots of candles in order to create the right ambiance.

While I was bustling about for the holidays, George was seated
on our sofa in the den with his computer in his lap. He has the

uncanny ability to tune out all noises and activities surrounding him and focus on one major thing at a time. I have the ability to move around our house doing several things at once. It may seem as though I'm not purposeful in my rushing around, but I have everything organized all within my holiday-planning brain. We were continuing to sip coffee while enjoying a few days together before the Christmas festivities began. We were to have a more intimate gathering for Christmas with only our two sons, John Mark and James. Our daughter, Jessica, was enjoying Christmas vacation in Belgium while visiting George's brother, Roy, who was stationed there.

Our hearts were heavy for Jessica. Just six weeks earlier, her husband of six years had announced his decision to end their marriage. Devastated does not even begin to describe the state of our daughter's heart from such a cruel blow. It was an exceptionally sad time for our entire family. John Mark and James were so hurt for their sister. George and I were torn between our extreme grief for our daughter, Jessica, and also our desire to repay our future ex-son-in-law for our daughter's broken heart and his reckless actions.

Like many women faced with this same scenario, Jessica was an amazing wife. She cooked, cleaned, worked hard, and accomplished much. She was continually affirming her husband and rarely spoke a negative word against him. We began noticing his increasingly selfish behavior and slight pulling away from our once-close family gatherings. We understand that marriages go through times of ups and downs, but we were shocked at his seemingly sudden decision.

Knowing that the holidays would be tough for Jessica, George suggested that she use her Christmas break from teaching to travel to her Uncle Roy's home in Belgium for a much-needed time of retreat and refocus. Roy, being the Henderson man that he is, would lovingly share the sites of Europe with her and provide sound advice. It was almost as if George and I also could take a mental vacation, knowing that Jessica apparently was having needs met in her own life for the first time since her six-year marriage started.

Our oldest son and middle child, John Mark, and our youngest son, James, both lived in the area, and both were out of the nest, although they both had nearby apartments. George and I were figuring out what it really meant to be empty nesters. While being an empty nester was sad at first, the realization of a kitchen that remained clean, refrigerator that remained stocked, and laundry room that actually had time to gather dust was becoming more and more appealing. It was the beginning of a new and exciting chapter.

James had just celebrated his nineteenth birthday two weeks earlier. He was going to college, living on his own, paying rent, and enjoying his bachelor lifestyle. In an overall effort to be healthier, he had begun a new workout routine and meal plan. We were really proud of him on all fronts.

After a couple of weeks of his new workout plan, James began complaining of backache. He would come over and let George examine the area. George, who is a former rugby coach and has done extensive weightlifting since his early twenties, would give him advice on how to lift weights differently. Convinced that James had simple muscular pain, he advised him of how to care for the pain and condition his body.

Over the next few weeks, the back pain continued and had even worsened. James then resorted to massage therapy to try and alleviate the problem. He rested from weightlifting, tried sleeping in different positions, and took anti-inflammatory medications in order to relieve the pain.

One afternoon, a few days before Christmas, while George and I were out enjoying lunch, James called. His back pain was not getting better; in fact, he said it was getting much worse. He was almost in tears as he described the level of pain he was experiencing. We suggested that he go to the nearest weekend clinic to have things checked out. Convinced it was something simple, we continued having lunch, but we were curious about James' pain level. We wondered whether he had a slipped disc or a torn muscle.

James called to give us the report from the clinic. The doctor thought he might possibly have a kidney stone or a gall stone. They arranged for an ultrasound to be performed at a nearby emergency room. We left the restaurant and met James at the hospital emergency room. He was pale and experiencing lots of pain. Typical to most emergency rooms, we had to fill out lots of paperwork and patiently wait to be seen.

While we were waiting, I decided my time would be better spent at home, preparing soup and getting our guest room ready for James. If indeed he had a kidney stone, he would need the comforts of home for a few days while he recovered. I left George and James together at the hospital and went home to make the necessary preparations.

I quickly moved into mom mode after I arrived home from the hospital. I changed clothes, put on my apron, and was prepared for action. I began taking things out of the freezer, chopping vegetables, and making some meals that James would enjoy. I called my mom and dad and told them about James' impending ultrasound. I continued my multimeal preparation while waiting to hear from George.

About an hour passed when the phone rang. I quickly answered and asked George what the ultrasound revealed. I wondered whether James had gall stones or kidney stones, or whether it was something else. George paused for a moment, then spoke quietly as he said, "Steph, they want to perform an MRI. The ultrasound revealed spots on James' spleen." I said, "What are the spots from? Do they know?" George

> "Steph, they want to perform an MRI. The ultrasound revealed spots on James' spleen."

said, "I'm not sure, and they are doing further tests to find out." At that moment, I felt like my heart sank to my feet. After a few seconds of silence, I said, "I'm on my way," and I hung up the phone.

I stood in the kitchen stunned. I wanted to cry, but I couldn't. I wanted to try to comprehend what this could mean, but I couldn't wrap my mind around what George had just shared. I knew enough to know that the further tests were to rule out something serious. I walked into my closet and began to stare at my clothes, trying to decide what I should wear to return to the hospital. I stood there just staring for several minutes—which at the time felt like several hours—trying to comprehend George's news. I was scared and shocked and in my heart said, "God, please, let my baby be okay." I finally snapped myself out of standing motionlessly in my closet and quickly grabbed a running suit, put my hair in a ponytail, and headed for the door.

During my drive to the hospital, I began praying and asking God to give me a word to bring peace to my heart. The Lord was quiet and so was I. I began searching through the CDs and radio stations, wanting desperately to hear a worship song that would speak to what I was feeling. I wanted God to send a song to me that had the message of, "Everything is going to be fine." I couldn't find one. In my search for music to minister during my drive, a new song that I'd heard several times before came on the station. I recognized the song's melody before the words began. I was relieved to find something that would bring peace to my troubled heart. When the words finally faded into the music, I began to cry when I remembered it was Kari Jobe's song, "Healer."

> You hold my every moment.
> You calm my raging seas.
> You walk with me through fire,
> and heal all my disease.
> I trust in you.
> I trust in you.

As the words continued, I knew that the news we would receive regarding James would not be what we expected. Through this song, God was preparing my heart. I continued to pray while driving to the hospital. The Lord spoke and said, "Stephanie, I trust you with this. You can trust me."

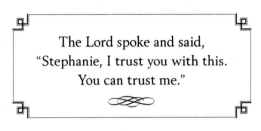

The Lord spoke and said, "Stephanie, I trust you with this. You can trust me."

I arrived at the hospital and found the room where James and George were waiting for the MRI test. James was lying in the hospital bed with George at his side. When I entered the room, I hugged both George and James and asked for the latest news. George began filling me in on everything they had been told. I tried to process what he was saying, but it was like my brain would not engage, and everything felt fuzzy. As we were discussing the details, I couldn't help but continually watch James' face and George's expression to try and read the situation more clearly.

After George finished sharing, we quietly sat together. James broke the silence when he looked at me and said, "Mom, do you think I have cancer?" My heart was pierced with his question. I could see the concern in his face. I held his hand and said, "I don't know, son." George grabbed my hand and laid his hands on James and began to pray. We cried, prayed, and asked God for peace, protection, and healing over James' body.

The technician came in and wheeled James out of the room for the MRI test. As the door closed, George and I began to talk. I said, "I think he's sick, honey." George slowly shook his head in agreement, and we began to cry, although we were holding out for the possibility that we were wrong. We sat quietly and prayed while James' test was performed.

After the test, the technician returned James to the room. The doctors had given him a good amount of pain medicine in order to alleviate his back pain, so he was asleep. He continued to sleep as George and I held hands and remained quiet.

The door to the hospital room swung open with the emergency room doctor and his assistant. They closed the door behind them, which I knew meant our news was not good. The doctor pulled up a stool, sat next to James, and said, "James, I have bad news. You have cancer. We believe you have Hodgkin's lymphoma, and I'm very sorry." I was watching my son's big brown eyes fill with tears as he received this news. We were stunned. The doctor continued, "The good news is that your cancer is very treatable, so if you have to have cancer, this is the one you want. We're going to make an appointment for you with an oncologist in a couple of days, and he will care for you." I wish I had words to describe how we felt when we received James' diagnosis. Sometimes, there just are no words, and this was one of those occasions.

We asked questions and tried to take everything the doctor was sharing in as best we could. The doctor and his assistant left the room so we could have some time alone.

We wept, hugged each other, and cried together. George stood over James and prayed over him, weeping and asking God to heal our son. I couldn't pray. My heart was broken for my son. We composed ourselves as a technician arrived in our room. They had to take some more blood work from James. They gave us several papers for follow-up and released us to go home.

We drove home from the hospital completely silent. I remember wanting to say something that would make the situation better, but I had no words. George, being the strong, silent type was quiet, but focused. James was sitting in the backseat of the car also quiet. I honestly was afraid to turn and look at him, because I didn't want to start crying and upset him more. We drove and didn't say a word out loud, but in our hearts we were constantly praying to God.

I suddenly began to hear music. Thinking that my radio station was still on, I began adjusting the buttons to turn them off. The sound continued, and I realized that the sound was from the backseat of our car. James was singing. As I pressed my ear to listen more carefully, I recognized the song, which was "Healer." The lyrics were

> I believe you're my healer,
> I believe you are all I need.
> I believe you're my portion.
> I believe you're more than enough for me.
> Jesus, you're all I need.

George and I both began to cry. James was singing the chorus of the same song God gave me earlier while proclaiming his faith in the darkest hour.

Christmas Eve

On Christmas Eve, we were in the oncology office for our follow-up appointment from the emergency room visit. The room was filled with mostly elderly people from all walks of life. James was by far the youngest patient in the room. We met with James' new doctor, Dr. Matthew Logsdon, who explained in detail about James' diagnosis. All the while, I kept looking around and thinking, "We do not belong here. This cannot be happening to our son." It was a time mixed with grief, disbelief, shock, and sadness.

Following the oncology appointment, we had a brief time together with our son, John Mark, before collapsing for the night. John Mark's heart was broken, and we were all trying to make sense of something that had no reason that we could find. We also had to call our daughter in Belgium and share the news with her. She was crushed and ready to come home and be with her family.

That night when George and I went to bed, I lay there hoping that when I awoke Christmas morning, this diagnosis would all be just a very bad nightmare. George wrapped his arms around me and whispered in my ear, "We're going to make it through this—somehow." I started to cry and felt like my heart was breaking.

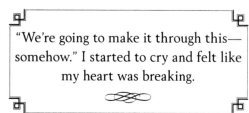

"We're going to make it through this—somehow." I started to cry and felt like my heart was breaking.

George woke up a few hours later and went downstairs to check on James, who was sleeping soundly. George gently laid his hands on James and began to pray over him. At first, he prayed for God to remove this situation from James' life. In the midst of his prayer, the Lord spoke to George's heart and said, "Do not pray for this to be removed. Pray that I will be glorified in all of you through this trial. I trust you with this."

George began to weep, and then he started to pray for God's glory to be revealed in James' life. He knew that this season would be a journey rather than a sprint and that God's glory would be the end result. He quietly returned to bed to try to get some sleep.

I awoke around three o'clock in the morning and could not go back to sleep. My mind was reeling from the events of the past several days. I was reliving the news of James' diagnosis and the plethora of information we had just received from the oncologist. I felt overwhelmed, to say the least. As I was praying, I heard the Lord whisper to me, "Stephanie, get up. I have a word for you."

Having known the Lord for many years, I was very familiar with times when the Lord "had a word for me." It usually meant that God wanted to speak to my heart about something specifically, whether it concerned vision for the future or a life rope to hang on while going through a trial. To be completely honest, I didn't want to know what the Lord had to say to me. I was afraid it would be more bad news. I tried and tried to go back to sleep, but without success. The Lord continued to speak to my heart saying, "Stephanie, get up. I have a word for you."

I very reluctantly crawled out of bed, trying not to wake George. As I walked down the stairs, I met twinkling lights that reflected off the perfectly tied bows on the gifts under our Christmas tree. The tree was lit beautifully, the presents wrapped; the bows on the garland beautifully tied, and the scent of the live evergreen tree filled the room. I reached for my Bible and took a seat in my favorite chair, which was positioned next to the Christmas tree. I sat there for several minutes and finally said, "Okay Father, I am here, and I'm ready."

I opened my Bible and the pages fell to 1 Samuel, Chapter 1. I was very familiar with this text because of teaching it many, many times. I began to weep when I saw the passage, because I already knew the story.

I read the story of Hannah, the wife of Elkanah, and her passion to have a child. Her prayer was not answered immediately, and year after year she petitioned the Lord to remember her and not forget her desire for a son.

I was sitting still and waiting for God to bring the word He wanted me to have from this text. The verse that caught my attention from this text was, I Samuel 1:28 (NLT) "Now I am giving him to the Lord and he will belong to the Lord his whole life."

At that moment, the Lord spoke to my heart and said, "Steph, Samuel's whole life, means *all* the days of his life. Every day of James' life belongs to me, and you need to surrender him to me, no matter what."

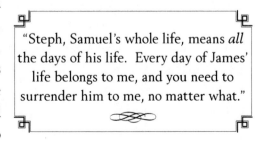

"Steph, Samuel's whole life, means *all* the days of his life. Every day of James' life belongs to me, and you need to surrender him to me, no matter what."

I began to weep as I meditated on this truth from the Lord. I knew that God was going to bring James through a journey and was going to work mightily through this situation. I needed to surrender to God's plan for James to walk out his destiny.

As I sat there and soaked in this concept, the Lord reminded me of something I had forgotten. The Lord said to me, "Stephanie, look around and tell me what you see." I looked around the room and didn't see anything out of the ordinary. The Christmas tree was lit with the packages arranged underneath—it was a beautiful picture of Christmas celebration. I continued to search my heart for what the Lord wanted to bring to my attention. As I was looking at the tree and lights, I suddenly remembered something I had forgotten that happened nineteen years ago.

Nineteen years earlier, I was seated by our Christmas tree. I had a new baby, James, that was two weeks old, and I was awake in the middle of night, rocking him back to sleep. While sitting up with James, quietly rocking and singing to him while he slept, the Lord spoke to my heart. The Lord gave me a special verse that night—from 1 Samuel, Chapter 1, where Hannah rejoices over her child being born and then surrenders her child to the Lord for his whole life (I Samuel 1:28) (NLT)

As tears rolled down my face with this memory, I was also reminded prior to becoming pregnant with James that I was scheduled for a full hysterectomy because of health problems I was experiencing. Two weeks before going into surgery to resolve these issues, a final ultrasound revealed that I was perfectly healthy. God healed me. Within six months, I became pregnant with James. Two weeks following his birth, on Christmas Eve, I held my new baby and felt completely overwhelmed at God's healing in my life and the precious gift of this boy for whom I prayed.

While the memory of this sweet night played in detail through my mind, the Lord spoke further and said, "Even though you had forgotten this, I have not forgotten. I have not forgotten James, either."

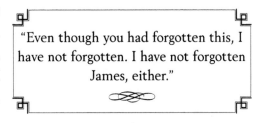

"Even though you had forgotten this, I have not forgotten. I have not forgotten James, either."

This same little baby was now a man, facing the challenge of his life. God reminded me that He has not moved or changed His mind about James' miraculous purpose. My job was to commit him to the Lord—*all the days of his life,* and trust the Lord, who miraculously healed me nineteen years ago, and who would also perform miraculous healing in my son's life.

The past two years while James has undergone treatment for cancer, God has continued to teach me how to behave as His daughter and trust His heart, even though I didn't understand His plan. I have called this season, "Daughterhood 101" because it has been a time of reframing my view of God and also the way God views me.

I have loved you, my people, with an everlasting love.
With unfailing love I have drawn you to myself.

Jeremiah 31:3 (NIV)

3

THE SWEET ADOPTION PROCESS

UNFORGETTABLE

THE SWEET
Adoption
PROCESS

Webster's Dictionary defines adoption as:

a·dopt ⊠ (a-dop-shun)[1]
tr.v. a·dopt·ed, a·dopt·ing, a·dopts
1. To take into one's family through legal means and
raise as one's own child.

*T*his chapter shares two adoption stories, which are both special
to me for many reasons. These real-life encounters have helped
me understand more deeply the sweet process of adoption.

Tom and Bekah Martinez

Roughly twenty years ago in New Orleans, Louisiana, during
Mardi Gras, police were on full alert to monitor drunken brawls,
women disrobing for beads, and the wildest array of costumes and
ensure everything was in order. New Orleans during Mardi Gras
season, especially in the French Quarter, is full of chaos, confusion,
drunkenness, and debauchery. In particular, this area during the

---

[1]   Miriam-Webster's Dictionary

Mardi Gras season has people who abandon any self-restraint during the parade season. On this night twenty years ago, the very smell of the city was detestable as people smoked, urinated in the streets, vomited from their binge drinking, and threw so much trash on the ground that at times the street asphalt was indistinguishable.

A variety of ministries often came into town during the Mardi Gras season to share the love of Jesus in the midst of such craziness. One ministry leader, who was most faithful to travel to New Orleans for ministry was a gentleman named Brent. Brent portrayed Jesus while carrying a cross and shared the message of Christ with anyone who would listen. This audience was extremely difficult to get through as people threw things at him, cursed, spat on him, and disrespected him. However, Brent's desire to see people come to know Christ was stronger than the level of disrespect he received.

During one of the days he was ministering in the French Quarter, a woman approached him with a rather odd request. In her arms she held a six-week-old baby boy, wrapped in a blanket. She asked Brent, "Would you please take care of my baby? I cannot care for him." She then placed in Brent's arms a little, strawberry blonde–haired, blue-eyed infant. She said, "I want to give my child to Jesus. I know you will take care of him."

The team that was accompanying Brent spoke with her at length, and she was indeed sober and serious about her request. She provided her contact information with the team and tearfully walked away from both Brent and her baby.

Brent returned to the ministry headquarters with the infant and thought that if she would agree to the legal adoption process, he would accept this as God's will for his wife and him to adopt this little baby boy. Word spread around our congregation about this little miracle baby that appeared out of the chaos of Mardi Gras. People began gathering much needed baby supplies for the newest member of Brent's family.

At our next church service, Brent and his wife sat in service with this beautiful, little, strawberry blonde–haired, blue-eyed boy in the infant carrier sitting on the pew. I remember distinctly watching them with this new baby. What also caught my attention was a couple in our church, Tom and Bekah, who were seated directly behind them.

Tom and Bekah attempted for years to have a baby without success. I specifically noticed Bekah. As she stood and gazed at the child, tears streamed down her face. I knew her heart was breaking over the strong desire to have a child, especially after seeing someone basically give her child to this family. My heart was broken for her and Tom.

Tom and Bekah spoke with Brent and his family after the service. They told them that if Brent and his family had any doubt about adopting this new baby that they would gladly adopt him. They shared their story of desperately wanting a child. These two families stood together and prayed for God's wisdom and for the desires of Tom and Bekah's hearts to be realized.

Brent and his wife left this encounter with Tom and Bekah. They continued to pray about this situation and sensed that the Lord was directing them to allow Bekah and Tom to adopt this little miracle baby. They called them and shared what God had placed on their hearts, but they explained that the child would have to go to the hospital and be examined, and the mother would have to sign the necessary legal papers to release custody.

The legal process was quickly set in place, and Bekah and Tom gripped faith through the days, surrounding what could be the realization of their dreams. Many factors could still threaten this process. They guarded their hearts as best they could, but they hoped with faith that this was God's intention to give them the child they spent years praying for. The mother agreed to all legal documents, and the hospital pediatricians completed the various tests to assure the child's health.

Five days after this process began, my phone rang and on the other end was Tom. Through tears he said, "Steph, we're going to the hospital to pick up *our* son." I wept with him and stood in awe as only God could orchestrate the circumstances in this couple's life.

I hurried to the local party store and drove to their house to place blue and white balloons on their porch and a "welcome baby boy" wreath on their front door. Many of our friends also gathered in excitement to greet the newest member of their family.

Friends and family welcomed Tom and Bekah home with plenty of cheers, claps, and tears of joy. This little baby boy, now named Steven, had a new home and loving parents. If all of this wasn't enough, Steven looks much like Bekah, who also has strawberry red hair and beautiful blue eyes.

George Henderson

I was married for almost twenty years to the most amazing man. John Guerra erupted in my heart and life very suddenly in 1983. Within one week of dating, he proposed and asked me to marry him. Knowing that this was God's man for me, I excitedly said, "Yes!" We shocked our parents, family, and friends, to say the least. In our immature hearts, we had no idea what our life would look like together, but we knew that we did not want to ever be apart. Together we began a journey as husband and wife. He was a pastor, and we worked in ministry together. We saw the miraculous birth of three very special children, Jessica, John Mark, and James. John's infectious humor made him a special person, and we and many of the people in our congregation loved him. He was a man who loved God deeply and sacrificially loved his family. He embraced the relationships in his life with much love and lots of humorous sarcasm as well.

John was diagnosed with a very aggressive form of leukemia on April 28, 2003. I remember receiving the diagnosis from the doctors at the hospital in New Orleans. I felt like I was in a movie, of sorts.

As the doctor shared this horrific diagnosis, I felt everything around me stop. His words, which were few, seemed like they went on for eternity in a very slow, almost dreamlike fashion. I remember having to steady myself against the hospital wall so I wouldn't collapse with this news. I was stunned, felt sick to my stomach, and felt very empty. I remember hearing the doctor continue explaining this diagnosis, but to this day I cannot tell you what he was saying. All I could imagine was how on earth I would share this with my then 12-, 17- and 18-year-old children.

The children joined us at the hospital as we shared this devastating news. I do not know a more helpless feeling than watching my children's faces as we tried our best to explain what we ourselves did not understand. We held hands, prayed, and proclaimed God's faithfulness even though we had no idea what we were facing. We were suddenly bombarded with tests, blood work, scans, and biopsies, all with the intent of having a clear diagnosis and course of treatment.

I remember standing in the oncology floor hallway, watching the various cancer patients walk up and down the hallways. They were bald from obvious chemotherapy treatments and walked, with an IV pole, slowly back and forth, over and over again. I remember praying and saying to God, "I just cannot see us doing this." God was silent.

"I just cannot see us doing this."
God was silent.

Over the course of the next forty-eight hours, we received news that given John's age, health, and course of treatment, the doctors felt confident he would recover. We were relieved with this news, and chemotherapy was scheduled to begin the next day.

The following day forever changed the course of my life and my children's lives. In what we thought was an optimistic future for this diagnosis ended with John's sudden death only three days after diagnosis. It all happened so suddenly that I had to go home and tell my children that their father was now in heaven.

Up until this point what I then knew of my relationship with God did not even bear weight on the grace, mercy, and strength that the Lord provided for me and my children. It truly was a time of heart-wrenching grief, accompanied by peace that truly "passes all understanding" like Philippians 4:7 says. Every day, we learned more about God's grace as He continued to heal our hearts.

As time progressed, God continued to heal us and give us a true heart of gratitude for the years that we had John. We completely loved each other and had no regret in our relationships. God continued to teach us all how to move forward in a way that honored the Lord and honored John as well.

I never imagined myself in another relationship, let alone married. I was content as a single mom and single woman. I had already experienced love that many never have the opportunity to experience. What could honestly top what I had?

I purchased a little five-pound Yorkie, which I named Zimoda, who became the delight of our home. Zimoda was a word that John crafted from his favorite beverage he had while doing ministry in Zimbabwe. It was a concoction of soda and juice that he named Zimoda, short for Zimbabwe soda. We thought it only fitting to give our new family mascot this name. We shortened his name to Moe.

We were grieving less and living more, and life became happier in our household. I remember feeling for the first time like I could actually breathe and that we could actually make it. I began writing a devotional at the time. I had no idea how to go about publishing or writing, but I just continued to journal my thoughts.

A friend of our family, George Henderson, was a marketing professional who attended our church. He was a special person for many reasons. First, he was the Boy Scout leader of my sons when they were young. Together he and John went on camp outings and adventures. George, with his steel blue eyes, also portrayed Jesus in our church's Christmas and Easter musical productions. He was also the much sought-after bachelor of the church. As an act of trying to do something kind for our family, he asked if he could help me market the devotional I was attempting to write. I quickly agreed because I had no idea what I was doing.

We began to meet for coffee and talk about the writing project. George was an interesting person who was well-traveled and loved extreme athletic sports. He has trekked Mount Everest for forty days, backpacked through the Mohave Desert, gone scuba diving in the Galapagos, sailed extensively, and summited some of the most aggressive mountains in Argentina and around the world. I was a little girl from Harahan, Louisiana, where the greatest adventure of my life was rolling down the levee as a child by the Mississippi River. I preferred high heels, polished nails, and styled hair that stayed in place to any outdoor activities that might cause me to sweat. George and I became great friends, and I appreciated the fact that he didn't treat me like a widow, but like a real person.

As our coffee exchanges continued over time, I realized that I looked forward to our times together. I remember specifically sitting in a nail salon where retro eighties music was playing and actually singing along with a love song and feeling joy in my heart—the first time in a long time.

One afternoon during our coffee exchanges, while seated outdoors, we were chatting, laughing, and talking about God, His plan, and the best way to market my devotional. I remember getting cold when the temperature dropped outside. George, being the gentleman that he is, took off the top layer of his sweater for me to use as a blanket. As he was pulling the sweater over his head and trying to keep his undershirt in place, I noticed the most amazing, rippled biceps. I felt like an Elvis fan when the women fainted after he threw his handkerchief into the audience. I am glad his sweater was over his head to hide my obvious "wow!" look on my face. I felt the heat of my embarrassment fill my face, and I tried desperately not to look flushed. Very awkwardly, I continued trying to talk and prayed for the conversation to end quickly.

I think I ran to my car and was so relieved to be out of what I felt was a spotlight on my experience. I remember talking to God on the way home and said, "*What* was that about? *Why* am I feeling like a 14-year-old girl who just realized that she had a crush on the neighbor next door?"

I did what any woman in my situation would do. I drove directly to my best friend, Mary's, house to tell her all about it. I knew that I could trust her with my heart and share the experience. I rushed into her house, and like two teenage girls we ran to her bedroom and locked the door. I started crying and said, "I don't know what's wrong with me!" We sat on an ottoman in her bedroom, and she listened lovingly as I tried to explain. I recalled the story for her and said, "His arms look like Hercules, and I think my knees buckled a bit."

Mary began crying, and said, "My friend, it's okay. It's okay to feel this way; we have seen this coming and could not be happier for you." Her husband Godi (who I am sure was listening at the door) then knocked and asked to come in. The two of them sat and assured me that it was time to enjoy what God may be leading me toward.

Over time, George and I began dating. We took our time and moved very slowly in this new relationship. Making sure that my children were on board with our relationship was very important to both of us. After two years of dating, George asked my father for my hand in marriage—and asked my children as well. We were married with all the children as attendants in our wedding.

Losing John was the greatest sorrow of my life. George was, by far, the greatest surprise of my life.

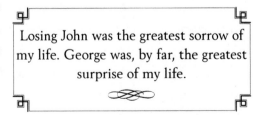

Losing John was the greatest sorrow of my life. George was, by far, the greatest surprise of my life.

We began our life together as a blended family. George did not have any children of his own and fully embraced my children as *our* children. George was a strong and very wise father. He intentionally developed unique relationships with each of the children. Doing so was easier than most, because he has known them since childhood. Over the course of years, our family grew and became more solid, both through victories and through trying times as well.

After roughly four years of marriage as a new family, we were making plans to celebrate George on Father's Day. Jessica and James were spending time, huddling and whispering. They also were making secret phone calls to John Mark, who was living in Hawaii at the time and serving a ministry internship. I knew they were all up to something, but I didn't know what it was. I tried to ask Jessica to reveal the secret, because she was the child who had the most difficulty keeping a secret. My attempt to discover their secret was unsuccessful, and I was happy to wait and see what they were planning.

On Father's Day, I prepared a meal fit for a king. One of our family traditions is for everyone to cook together in the kitchen. We were busy making appetizers, side dishes, desserts, and so on, for George's special day. When the meal was complete, we adjourned to the den for the presentation of gifts.

George is more of an introvert and would prefer to give gifts rather than receive. He humbly sat on the couch while I showered him with new wardrobe items for the summer. Jessica and James were seated across from us and were anxiously awaiting their turn to show George what they selected as his gift.

Jessica, being the oldest was the spokesperson for the children. James sat next to Jessica as she began sharing with George. Jessica said, "Pastor Brady has been preaching on orphans and widows, and it has really impacted us. We realize that while our biological father is in heaven, on this earth, we are orphans ... without a father. All of us have discussed it, and we would be honored if you, George, would adopt us as your legal children." With that announcement, Jessica and James handed George the adoption papers they and John Mark already completed to request to legally become his children.

My husband of few words and controlled emotions put his head down and started to weep. He was speechless. Through his tears, he said, "It would be my honor." I was also weeping and without words.

The years before our marriage, I was grieved that my children were without their biological father. I desperately wanted that place to be filled. I had no idea how God would fill it—until this day. They wanted to be adopted. In their words, "We know that our (biological) father is in heaven, but we want to have a dad on earth."

These two adoption accounts are very different, but they both represent the heart of the sweet adoption process. In Tom and Bekah's story, this beautiful adoption story illustrates to what measure God will move in order to bring about the desires He places in our hearts. Tom and Bekah could never have planned this journey, and yet, all the while, God had perfectly prepared and timed this adoption. God answered Tom and Bekah's many years of prayer with little Steven.

Tom and Bekah had no idea how God would respond to the desire of their heart to have a child. In the midst of the chaotic Mardi Gras season in New Orleans, God lovingly brought this miraculous gift of adoption.

This story additionally represents the heart of God in His relentless pursuit of us. Isn't it true that God's desire for relationship with us is not based on whether we are at our best or at a chaotic time in our own lives? Somehow we think to have a relationship with our father, God, we have to be cleaned up, with our life in order and tulips blooming behind the picket fences of our lives. The truth is that God wants us as a part of His family, no matter what.

His love transcends any amount of mess we may find ourselves in past, present, or future.

Putting the Past in the Past

One of the toughest parts of truly embracing the daughterhood in our relationship with God is allowing ourselves to leave the past *in* the past and realign our identity through the truth found in the Word of God. I've met countless women who have introduced themselves as, "Hi, my name is Sharon, and I've been divorced twice. It's nice to meet you." It's almost as if "and I've been divorced twice" is their last name. This declaration really saddens my heart because they typically are communicating a pain from the past. They fear being judged or marked by this terrible time that they have allowed to become their identity.

Let's be honest. We all experience disappointment in life. We all have faults, make mistakes, and have things that happen that we regret. I can think of many examples when I wished I had said or done something differently. I've regretted and feel ashamed for doing things; however, I've memorized 1 John 1:9 (NIV), which says, "If we confess our sins, [God] is faithful and just to forgive us our sins and cleanse us from all unrighteousness." Equally as important is not allowing consequences of other people's sin or poor choices define us of who we are.

I was a victim of sexual abuse in my childhood. Someone from outside my family horribly violated my innocence. Typical with most sexual abuse stories, the person threatened me not to tell my parents. My mom and dad were extremely careful, watchful parents, and they were deeply grieved when I finally told them about the abuse almost ten years later. Abusers are typically very manipulative and successful with using scare tactics in their abuse. Counseling has helped me heal the scars and helped me redefine who I am based on worth and value rather than through feeling dirty and unworthy. Healing from this type of violation can take years, and it's not been an easy path. Allowing God to redefine you through the truth in His word and by walking in freedom from the past is vital in embracing true daughterhood with Christ. We cannot let the titles or circumstances from the past define our future.

Not long after being widowed, I remember some people in the church who lovingly referred to me as, "the church widow." Their intentions were innocent, but wearing this label made me feel broken on the inside. God was doing a miraculous grief-healing in my life, and I didn't want to be referred to as the church widow. Besides, the word "widow" makes me think of spiders! Even though, when filling out paperwork, I had to check the little "widowed" box, I didn't want a word to define me. I wanted God to define me. He calls me "daughter."

We Need a Father

As reflected in the adoption story involving my family, we, as children, have a need for a Father. We want to feel protected, loved, and accepted.

In Galatians, Chapter 4, the Apostle Paul writes about the account of Jesus' birth. Jesus was born of the virgin, Mary, under the "conditions of law." This refers to the Old Testament reference in relationship to God. Before the birth, death, burial, and resurrection of Jesus, as told in the Gospels of the New Testament, the people would relate to God through offering animal sacrifices in order to atone for their sin. This atonement process was considered the law that many were still adhering to even after encountering Jesus. Paul describes the new way to have relationship with Jesus, which was set in place when Jesus willingly died on the cross and became the ultimate atonement and sacrifice for our sins. Because of this incredible act of mercy on our behalf, we now can enter into direct relationship with Jesus by adoption.

Galatians 4:4–7 (MSG) says

> But when the time arrived that was set by God the Father, God sent his Son, born among us of a woman, born under the conditions of the law so that he might redeem those of us who have been kidnapped by the law. Thus we have been set free to experience our rightful heritage. You can tell for sure that you are now fully adopted as his own children because God sent the Spirit of his Son into our lives crying out, "Papa! Father!" Doesn't that privilege of intimate conversation with God make it plain that you are not a slave, but a child? And if you are a child, you're also an heir, with complete access to the inheritance.

No matter where you have come from, who you are today, or what you've experienced in your life in the past, this passage says, "We have been set free to experience our *rightful* heritage." When we ask God to adopt us as His daughters, we no longer are bound to the path or nature we once realized. This powerful scripture says, *"We have been set free."* God's brand new, incredible heritage for us eternally trumps our past, present, failures, and memories. It's a fresh start.

Secondly, these verses teach that God has sent within us the "spirit of his Son into our lives." This is something we yearn for as we desire to have our Father, our Daddy relationship. God's spirit comes in, we have this incredible desire to have a relationship with God, and we are eternally fulfilled.

Having this internal desire for a father can only be met through a relationship with Jesus. No material objects or person can fill this void. It is a supernatural place meant only to be filled by our supernatural father. When we attempt to fill this void with things other than the presence of God, it creates a vacuum in our heart.

Imagine owning a clear, heart-shaped, glass vase. Imagine taking little pieces of paper and writing down all the things that are most important in your life. The different pieces may read job, children, finances, or appearance. Then, imagine taking all these pieces of paper and crumpling them and placing them in the heart-shaped vase. In order to fill every nook and cranny of the vase, you carefully compress the paper into all the various curves of the heart-shaped vase. After you're confident that you've completely filled the vase, you then take it and hold it up to the light. Through the illumination of your clear vase, you discover that even though you thought it was completely filled, you discover several hollow spots that the light now reveals.

Dissatisfied that your crumpled papers did not adequately fill the heart-shaped vase, you then find a pitcher of clean water. You pour all the clean water into the heart-shaped vase and realize that the water not only fills every part, but that it's now overflowing. You cannot find any hollow points.

In John 7:38 (NLT), God says, "Anyone who believes in me may come and drink! For the Scriptures declare, 'Rivers of living water will flow from his heart.'" When we try to fill the empty places of our hearts with people, items, or activities instead of God, we will always have hollow spots. However, as the verse says, "Rivers of living water will flow (abundantly) from our heart." God created our hearts with a desire for Him, as our Father. No substitutes will satisfy.

Are you adopted by the Lord? Have you asked Him to be your father? Are you unsure of your relationship with God? If not, take time now and ask. You can do this by simply praying a prayer, something like this:

Dear Jesus,

I realize I have not asked to be adopted by you, but now, I want to. I give you everything in my life that has defined me outside of your rightful heritage for me. I have not been perfect and ask you to forgive the sin in my life and give me a clean slate. Please teach me how to be your daughter and accept you as my Father whose love for me cannot be understood, but I accept it through faith. Help me to view myself as you see me and live my life differently from this day forward. Amen.

If you prayed this prayer and asked God to adopt you, He has heard your prayers and has welcomed you into the family as a new daughter! I am so excited for you! The word of God clearly states that not only do you become his daughter; he empowers you as his child. John 1:12 (NIV) says, "But as many as received him, to them gave the power to become the sons (daughters) of God, even to them that believe on his name"

Today truly is the first day of the rest of your life. God has come and filled all the hollow places that other things once attempted to fill. You are His daughter, and He is rejoicing in your new established relationship. I have written a special message for you located at the conclusion of this book (in chapter 10). Please email me at stephaniehendersonministries@gmail.com and let me know about this new relationship you have chosen with Christ.

If you are already a daughter, but realize you've defined yourself as something other than through God's rightful heritage for you, I encourage you to spend time in prayer asking God to help you see yourself as He sees you. Maybe you've tried to fill your heart with hollow things rather than a deeper relationship with Christ. God's grace and mercy is new every day. Let me challenge you to spend some time confessing areas where you have sought to fill the void in your life with other things rather than the presence of God. I first encourage you to take some time through prayer and put your relationship with Christ in its proper place. You also need to uproot destructive words that may have defined you, and labels or actions of others that may have stunted your spiritual growth. Whether through prioritizing your status in life or anything else that has kept you from behaving like His daughter, take time now to realign your life with God's plan for you.

Understanding the process by which you belong to God is important. Doing so helps you move from understanding who you are to *whose* you are. God has an eternal love for you, and His journey is the most exciting plan you could ever imagine.

> The Lord your God is in your midst, a mighty one who will save; he will rejoice over you with gladness; he will quiet you by his love; he will exult over you with loud singing.

> Zephaniah 3:17(NIV)

4

THE SLAVE-VERSUS-DAUGHTER MINDSET REVEALED

UNFORGETTABLE

THE SLAVE-VERSUS-DAUGHTER
Mindset
REVEALED

The Spirit of the Lord is upon me, because he has
anointed me to bring glad tidings to the poor. He has
sent me to proclaim liberty to captives and recovery of
sight to the blind, to let the oppressed go free.

Luke 4:18(NIV)

The famous movie, *Roots*, was filmed when I was in high
school. I remember nightly watching the miniseries and being
horrified with the reality of slavery that impacted generations. I still
remember the scenes where the slaves were in chains, sometimes
around their feet, hands, and even around their necks. I remember
being so sickened by the way they were treated. In many cases, the
owners had a sense of entitlement and acted as if the slaves should
have been grateful for their forced lifetime of service.

When you think of the slave-versus-daughter mindset, what do
you envision? If you're like me when I first began trying to grasp
daughterhood, you may be drawing a mental blank. To be honest, I
had no idea how to conceptualize this either because it was foreign
to the way I related to God for many years.

42

I had a very good relationship with the Lord. After experiencing the sudden loss of my late husband, John, I found myself coming to understand a new depth with the Lord. The truth is that I desperately needed God. I was suddenly thrust into a life as a single mom and had to bear the responsibility for our household and try to be strong while my children grieved.

Before this time, I considered myself to be an above-average Christian, based on the time I spent in my personal Bible study and time of prayer. Being in full-time ministry certainly lent itself to my continual growth as a believer. I have led worship, taught Bible study, sang in the church choir, volunteered to help the homeless, and participated in a myriad of countless service projects. I taught my first children's choir class when I was fourteen, and I was employed as a staff member of a church at eighteen. I've spent my life working in ministry and serving God.

Before I experienced extreme loss, my daily routine with God consisted of listening to Christian radio, reading a verse or chapter for the day, and praying. When my life suddenly changed and I found myself in the midst of such radical transformation, I realized that God was either going to be everything I knew that He could be or not. It was a crossroad for me.

I felt God's strength and peace during this time and could not understand it. I found myself making choices and leading my family, although this wisdom was foreign to what I had previously experienced. I felt so ill-equipped, and for the first time, I realized what it meant for God to truly be my portion. He became everything that I was not—and so much more. My prior five minutes of Scripture reading turned into reading the Scripture during the morning, noon, and night. My nighttime reading turned into me pouring over God's Word. I studied every person who suffered loss in the Bible to try and figure out how he or she had succeeded. My prayer time turned into spending a good part of the later nights on my knees, face down in my closet, not with a box of tissues, but with a towel that could absorb the sound of my crying (so my children did not hear). Each and every day God strengthened me and gave me hope and joy despite my immense grief.

When the Lord spoke to me in the Denver airport, I realized that even though my relationship with God had grown so tremendously, I still thought that I needed to do something in order to evoke God's favor and attention to situations of need in my life.

In other words, I thought that if I confessed my sins or fasted caffeine, I would somehow draw God's gaze to my situation so He could respond. What God has taught me since that day in the airport is that no number of tasks can make up for what He's already done for me. I've had His favor all along. I have been on a new path by taking my already intimate relationship with God to a new level by behaving like his daughter and remembering His great love for me.

The first step was learning about the difference between a slave and a daughter. This truth has transformed the way I serve and behave more than anything else.

Slave Mentality

In times past, a person would serve a family or business. The family or business would give the hired hand a place to live, three square meals a day, and a daily checklist of chores to be completed. The hired hand would wake up, look at the chore list for the day, and begin the assigned work. For this discussion, I assume the hired hand was working in an apple orchard, and her name was Sarah, because we are daughters.

Sarah began her day by eating the first meal provided and then going immediately to accomplish the list of daily tasks. Sarah walked to the apple orchard, picked up her bushel, and began filling her basket. When the lunch whistle rang, she was allowed to stop, sit by a tree, and eat what the owner prepared for her. After she completed lunch, she continued picking apples until the end of the day. At the completion of her day, she brought her bushel filled with apples to the owner, who weighed the bushel and gave her a crisp one dollar bill for a day's wages. She returned to her quarters, ate the meal prepared for her, and then retired to her bunk for the night. On the next day, she went through the very same actions. In fact, as a hired hand, she was assigned these tasks day after day after day and received a dollar at the end of every day for completing the daily tasks.

You may be wondering what any of this has to do with your slave-versus-daughter mindset. I did too, until I realized this behavior translated into modern-day terms.

Every Sunday, you wake up, eat breakfast, and get ready for church. You drive your car to your church of choice, park, walk inside to find your favorite spot to sit. You stand up, sing worship songs, and contribute to the offering to give a portion back to the Lord. You sit down, open your Bible, and listen to a sermon. At the end of the sermon, you pray together, shake hands with those around you, get back into your car, and go home. You have completed your Sunday tasks and done what you believe pleases God, and you get a check on your card at the end of the day (your dollar).

On Monday, you wake up and open your Bible to read a verse or two. You pray for the needs of the day and begin your daily routine. You might have worship music playing, or you might have Scripture cards in your office or in your car to remind you of God's Word. You pray over your lunch and continue the day's activities, trying to think good thoughts and do good actions. You go home, enjoy dinner together, praying before the meal, and relax by watching some television or reading a book. At the end of the day, you say your prayers and hope you've done enough to receive a check at the end of the day (another dollar).

On Tuesday, you wake up late and in a bad mood and have to forgo reading your Bible. You rush around trying to accomplish the duties of the day as best as you can. You look at the Scriptures posted in your office or car, which only serve as a reminder of how you've already failed for the day. Feeling badly, you say an extra long prayer at lunch, making sure your head is bowed longer so those individuals watching will, in your opinion, see Jesus in you. You return to your duties, feeling a little better because of your sacrificial lunch prayer and continue your day. You go home and eat dinner, again saying an extra long prayer because you blew it earlier in the morning, and then spend some time relaxing before you go to bed. Tonight, when you say your bedtime prayers, you confess how you've not measured up during the day. You get only a partial check mark (50 cents), and you promise to do better tomorrow.

On Wednesday, you wake up extra early and spend an additional ten minutes reading Scripture. You are determined to be back on your spiritual track today. You have loud worship music playing in your car and sing along all the way to the office. You greet everyone with a hearty "Hello and God bless you!" today because you are determined for your light to shine brighter than yesterday's day of storm and thunder. You smile as you look at the Scripture posted in your office or car because you know God must be happier with you today than He was yesterday. You enjoy your lunch and pray before you begin your meal so your powerful prayers can again impact those onlookers. You whistle as you walk out the door to return home for your nightly meal. You pray with boldness over your meal, thanking God for the day of success you've had. You take time to relax while feeling very fulfilled from the day's accomplishments, and then go to bed. At tonight's time of prayer, you are certain that you've received at least *two* checks for today! Satisfied with your achievement, you feel fulfilled and enjoy a peaceful night's sleep.

Say that you have several months or even years like this—daily checks, unchecks, rechecks—all doing the things that you believe will make God happy with you, day in and day out.

What happens, though, when your life goes in the proverbial ditch? For example, say you've had a good amount of time when you've received full checks for the day and suddenly life collapses. Maybe you've been fired from a job, had divorce papers served, had someone diagnosed with a terminal illness, or even worse.

How does your spiritual checklist measure against life's storms? Usually it will cause you to go back and reflect over the actions in your life. Although not perfect, you are sure you've attained an acceptable standard to God. You think, "How could this happen to *me*? I'm living right, I'm praying over my meals daily, I'm reading the word of God, I'm getting checks at the end of the day." You then may be tempted to measure yourself against others who you are certain have not received as many checks at the end of their days as you have. What about Mary? She cheats on her husband, constantly gossips, she doesn't pray over *any* of her meals, and she's healthy, employed, and married. At this point, you may begin to think, "This is not fair! I do not deserve this!"

The next day you wake up. You do not read God's Word; you don't pray over breakfast, lunch, or dinner; and you take down your Scripture reminders that you've previously posted. After all, what's the use? And sadly, in the core of your heart, you have spent time measuring your actions as a sort of hall pass from God for a life without heartache, pain, or stress. In your limited understanding, you feel like despite all your good works, God has failed you and even forgotten you.

What I have described is indeed a slave mindset. It is relationship with God built upon our ability to do something impossible— that is, be good enough or work hard enough in order to somehow gain the favor of God and a life without pain or suffering.

John 16:33 (NIV) reminds us, "I have told you these things, so that in me you may have peace. In this world you will have trouble. But take heart! I have overcome the world."

The truth is that you will have hardship in this life. Period. Pain is a common thread throughout humanity; it visits everyone. The slave mindset will foster an unhealthy, almost entitled attitude toward God as you expect His payment of "the good life" for your sacrificial actions.

The Daughter Mindset

The daughter mindset is one that is quietly confident that God is always working for her good, no matter what circumstances may represent otherwise. This understanding of the core value of God's heart requires a maturing process through an intentional relationship with God.

This mindset doesn't mean that you, as God's daughter, don't have times where you will struggle with feelings of doubt, fear, insecurity, or uncertainty. These feelings and emotions are part of being human. However, through the process of working through these times of doubt, which everyone faces, you come to the absolute conclusion that God will come through on your behalf and that you can rest in the truth that He will always keep His promises. His Word becomes the core by which you choose to believe the heart of God rather than follow your emotions or logic.

Does the daughter mindset include fasting, praying, giving, kindness, compassion, and caring? Of course it does. The difference is these attributes become a natural part of the daughter's heart because she knows her Father, knows His word, and desires to live a life that represents her heritage as His child. She does not need to do things in order to prompt God's favor. She realizes that she already has His favor and responds from a place of fullness rather than emptiness.

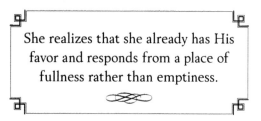

> She realizes that she already has His favor and responds from a place of fullness rather than emptiness.

John 16:33 (NIV) beautifully portrays the daughter mindset: "I have told you these things, so that in me you have peace" In this Scripture, you can see the relationship of the Father to his daughter.

The Father shares his secrets ("I have told you these things …") and she spends time listening to His wisdom.

While the Father's words are filled with wisdom, they are also filled with a strong, secure, protective nature of God ("Take heart! I have overcome the world."). In other words, God is saying, "Daughter, no matter what happens in life, through me, you will have peace and I will set the record straight in the happenings of this world."

A daughter mindset is one that is in tune with her Father; it has nothing to do with performance or perfection. The daughter mindset comes out of *fullness* from relationship where she spends time in prayer, because she trusts her Father's heart to take care of her needs. She reads His Word because she knows that His words are sharper than any two-edged sword and provides everything she needs. She posts Scriptures around her office or car as love notes from a Father who wants her to succeed and thrive in her destiny. She attends church, worships, gives, and enjoys the sermon because she knows that being with others who also love the Father enriches her life. She enjoys worship music because it is a melodious reminder of the truths of her Father's heart.

And when the daughter's life goes into the proverbial ditch, she runs trustingly into her Father's arms because she knows that *He* is her refuge.

> And when the daughter's life goes into the proverbial ditch, she runs trustingly into her Father's arms because she knows that *He* is her refuge.

The daughter lifestyle has no checks or dollars at the end of the day because she realizes, as shared in Galatians 4:7 (MSG), that she already owns it all. "And if you are a child, you're also an heir, with complete access to the inheritance."

Operating as a daughter means you operate out of your abundance and fullness rather than out of what you perceive you are lacking.

You serve God, you use your gifts for Him, and you minister to others because you have an overflowing heart of gratitude, trust, and relationship.

God does not give you a checklist to accomplish, but a race to run. He has an amazing destiny planned for you that simply requires your obedience and relationship.

5

THE UNFORGETTABLY PERSISTENT HANNAH

UNFORGETTABLE

THE UNFORGETTABLY
Persistent
HANNAH

We are made to persist. That's how we find out
who we are.

—Tobias Wolff

I have a very loving father who has always been a kind and
compassionate man. He has been a wonderful earthly figure
of my Heavenly Father and I'm thankful for that.

One Mother's Day, following our church service, we went out to
eat and celebrate Mom. I was about six years old at the time. This
occasion was very special, and Mom appreciated the opportunity
to have some time away from the kitchen. A long line of people
were waiting to get into the restaurant, and we waited outside for
what seemed like an eternity, especially for a hungry six-year-old.
My parents were always very careful to keep us close at hand, and
I held my dad's hand while we waited in line. I remember the
summer weather was hot and humid, and I wished that I was not
dressed in church clothes. Every few minutes, I would release my
father's hand in order to wipe off the accumulating sweat from

52

my tiny fingers. Somehow in the midst of one of my sweat-wiping moments, I accidentally grabbed another man's hand to hold instead of my father's. I didn't immediately realize it and continued holding a strange man's hand while waiting in line. After a few minutes, I looked up to ask my Dad how much longer we would have to wait and was horrified to realize the hand I was holding was *not* my father's hand.

So many people surrounded me in my four-foot world of existence that I felt like I was lost in a giant's jungle. I quickly released the stranger's hand and began looking around saying, "Where is my dad? Where is *my* dad?" Through my panicked state and through the multitude of people, I suddenly saw a large hand, reaching through the crowd, and a voice, calling my name, "Stephanie! Stephanie!" I looked up and saw my dad who had been searching for me. With relief, I grabbed his big, strong hand and did not let it go again—not even to wipe off the sweat.

Have you ever felt lost or forgotten? Have you ever spent time wondering if God sees you or even cares about you? Have you ever had something that you needed so desperately and wondered where God was? Probably everyone has felt that way at one time or another.

Hannah can relate. Hannah, the wife of Elkanah, had a desperate situation, which for years she persistently prayed. Interestingly enough, but not uncommon in the society of those times, Elkanah had a second wife named Peninnah. The book of 1 Samuel 1–20 (NIV) shares Hannah's story:

> There was a certain man from Ramathaim, a Zuphitefrom the hill country of Ephraim, whose name was Elkanah son of Jeroham, the son of Elihu, the son of Tohu, the son of Zuph, an Ephraimite. He had two wives; one was called Hannah and the other Peninnah. Peninnah had children, but Hannah had none.

Year after year this man went up from his town to worship and sacrifice to the Lord Almighty at Shiloh, where Hophni and Phinehas, the two sons of Eli, were priests of the Lord. Whenever the day came for Elkanah to sacrifice, he would give portions of the meat to his wife Peninnah and to all her sons and daughters. But to Hannah he gave a double portion because he loved her, and the Lord had closed her womb. Because the Lord had closed Hannah's womb, her rival kept provoking her in order to irritate her. This went on year after year. Whenever Hannah went up to the house of the Lord, her rival provoked her till she wept and would not eat. Her husband Elkanah would say to her, "Hannah, why are you weeping? Why don't you eat? Why are you downhearted? Don't I mean more to you than ten sons?"

Once when they had finished eating and drinking in Shiloh, Hannah stood up. Now Eli the priest was sitting on his chair by the doorpost of the Lord's house. In her deep anguish Hannah prayed to the Lord, weeping bitterly. And she made a vow, saying, "Lord Almighty, if you will only look on your servant's misery and remember me, and not forget your servant but give her a son, then I will give him to the Lord for all the days of his life, and no razor will ever be used on his head."

As she kept on praying to the Lord, Eli observed her mouth. Hannah was praying in her heart and her lips were moving but her voice was not heard. Eli thought she was drunk and said to her, "How long are you going to stay drunk? Put away your wine."

"Not so, my lord," Hannah replied, "I am a woman who is deeply troubled. I have not been drinking wine or beer; I was pouring out my soul to the Lord. Do not take your servant for a wicked woman; I have been praying here out of my great anguish and grief."

Eli answered, "Go in peace, and may the God of Israel grant you what you have asked of him."

She said, "May your servant find favor in your eyes." Then she went her way and ate something, and her face was no longer downcast.

Early the next morning they arose and worshiped before the Lord and then went back to their home at Ramah. Elkanah made love to his wife Hannah, and the Lord remembered her. So in the course of time Hannah became pregnant and gave birth to a son. She named him Samuel, saying, "Because I asked the Lord for him." I Samuel 1:20 (NIV)

I love this story of Hannah. Notice in the account that Hannah repeatedly prays, weeps, and petitions the Lord for the ability to have a child. Her husband, Elkanah, attempts to console her by saying, "Am I not more than ten sons to you?" Although Hannah loved her husband, the desire to have a child seemed to almost consume her.

As if her barren state was not overwhelming enough, she had a rival in wife No. 2 who constantly reminded her of her perceived shortcoming. The Priest Eli also mistook her desperation for drunkenness.

As I have studied this passage, it struck me the number of times Hannah refers to being "forgotten" by the Lord or asks God to "remember" her. Although you may not have experienced being married to man with more than one wife, having a priest mistake your petitions as drunkenness, or having gone to the mountain to sacrifice yearly, you can probably relate to the feeling of being forgotten.

Through leading women's conferences, I have the honor of meeting all types of women. These women come from all seasons and stages of life. One area we all have in common is the struggle of faith in understanding that we truly matter to God. When times are good, this concept is easier to embrace. However, when life's storms roll in, which they often do, really embracing God's love and belief in His faithfulness becomes harder.

What do you do, when like Hannah, you have a aching in your heart; whether from loss, failure, disappointment, or unmet needs? How do you, in the midst of trials, continue to stand in faith that your Father (Daddy) has not forgotten about you or the need in your life? How do you continue to behave as a daughter in these times of doubt?

The answer is in persistence, by which I mean, continuing to press through your natural responses by believing that your Father will not let you down. Notice in Hannah's story, she persists. The Scripture says, "year after year" Hannah petitioned the Lord to fulfill this desire in her life. It wasn't a day, a week, or even a month—it was over the course of years. All the while, she stood in faith that God had not forgotten the importance of this request.

At times I will pray, share a need with God, and watch it fulfilled almost before I say "amen." However, other times the answers don't come immediately. The moments of prayer can turn into days, weeks, months, or years. I can easily believe that God is not interested in meeting the needs of my heart. Equally seductive can be the temptation to step outside of this faith and try to attain God's favor by fasting, praying, or doing sacrificial things in order to somehow evoke God's attention (the slave mentality). Believe me, if by doing acts of service had the ability to alleviate pain in my life and in the life of my family and friends, I would do it! The truth is that while seasons in our life do require fasting and prayer, they are never meant to be used as tools to somehow convince God or try to manipulate Him to move on our behalf or to move in the way we desire. Standing in faith, in persistence, is the relational response as a daughter to our heavenly Father, whom we trust.

When I am waiting for God's response, I am usually not aware of all the ways He is busy working behind the scenes to set the stage for answering my prayers. While we have been on the journey to see our son James healed from cancer, we have had many opportunities where this waiting on God's healing has been tested.

James had just completed a round of new chemotherapy drugs with the hopes that he would be in remission. He had scheduled a positron emission tomography (PET) scan, and my heart was hopeful that the results would be good. Because I was still coming to understand how to behave as a daughter, I have constantly been asking God for wisdom. The peace that God has provided has been incredible. As God has taught me to relinquish fear and embrace persistent faith, the result has been transforming.

The results came and were not what we wanted or expected. The PET scan showed slight improvement in one area, but it was not improved in the other area where the cancer was growing. It was disappointing to say the least. In my effort to try and understand the results of this test, I went to God in prayer. I cried and asked God, "Why?' I stumbled in my faith and wanted to understand. As I remained quiet after sharing my heart with God, He responded. God whispered, "Stephanie, the right answer at the wrong time is not the right answer. My ways and timing are perfect. Keep trusting me."

> God whispered, "Stephanie, the right answer at the wrong time is not the right answer. My ways and timing are perfect. Keep trusting me."

That word impacted me. It gave me hope because I knew the right answer was coming. It caused my heart to sink because I knew this battle was not yet over. It challenged the warrior in me to continue to press and persist until the right time and right answer arrived.

Please do not think that I am expressing in any way, shape, or form that this progression is easy. Although this process is heart-wrenching at times, equally important is resisting my enemy's lies who whispers in my ears that God has forgotten me and my child.

In times like this, I have to put aside my natural responses, and as a daughter, stand firm on the Word of God, trusting what I cannot yet see.

As Isaiah 49:15b–16a (NIV) says, "I will not forget you! See, I have engraved you on the palm of my hands." I love this verse. God has engraved us (carved, tattooed) on the palm of his hands. This Scripture references a covenant made in the Old Testament. When an agreement was made, the people would actually carve the contract into their hands as a symbol of their commitment. God uses this common Jewish practice to relate His covenant with us. He has carved our names in the palm of his hands—a symbol of His inability to ever forget His commitment to us.

In times of doubt or despair, you can confidently rest in the fact that God hears you and delights in giving you the desires of your heart. You have to simply be patient and trust that God is, as His words says in Romans 8:28 (NIV), "Working all things together for good for those who love God and are called according to His purpose." Hannah's story serves as such inspiration for you as you wait on God to respond to your prayers.

Do you have a "Samuel" prayer? Are there circumstances or situations you are waiting for God's response? Is it the reconciliation of relationships? Is it healing of your heart? Is it a financial crisis that you need God's rescue?

No matter what your "Samuel" petition might include, trust that God is going to bring the right answer, at the right time. The answer may not present itself as you imagine, but it will always be for your good and for His glory.

Maybe while waiting, like my six-year-old experience, you've grabbed onto the wrong hand in the process. Trying to fill unmet needs or dashed expectations with things or people other than God can be an easy but unfulfilling. The beautiful truth about grace and forgiveness is that as a daughter, you have access to new beginnings daily.

Remember, the same God who has carved your name in the palm of His hand is also reaching for you and calling you by name. He loves you more than you can imagine.

Scriptures on Praying with Persistence

Always be joyful. Keep on praying. No matter what happens, always be thankful, for this is God's will for you who belong to Christ Jesus.

1 Thessalonians 5: 16–18 (NLT)

Don't worry about anything; instead, pray about everything. Tell God what you need, and thank him for all he has done. If you do this, you will experience God's peace, which is far more wonderful than the human mind can understand. His peace will guard your hearts and minds as you live in Christ Jesus.

Philippians 4:6–7(NLT)

Trust in the Lord with all your heart; do not depend on your own understanding. Seek his will in all you do, and he will direct your paths.

Proverbs 3:5–6 (NLT)

"Pray like this: Our Father in heaven, may your name be honored. May your Kingdom come soon. May your will be done here on earth, just as it is in heaven. Give us our food for today, and forgive us our sins, just as we have forgiven those who have sinned against us. And don't let us yield to temptation, but deliver us from the evil one."

Matthew 6:9–13 (NLT)

6

THE UNFORGETTABLY COURAGEOUS JOCHEBED

UNFORGETTABLE

THE UNFORGETTABLY
Courageous
JOCHEBED

Courage is not the absence of fear, but rather the
judgment that something else is more important than fear.

—Ambrose Redmoon

*J*ochebed is not a biblical name that many people recognize. In
fact, she is not named in this text at all. The Scripture later
gives her name. However, most people are very familiar with her
story, because she is the mother of Moses.

Her courageous story unfolds in Exodus 1–2:10 (NIV)

> Now a new king arose over Egypt who did not know
> Joseph and he said to his people, "Behold the people of
> the sons of Israel are mightier than we. Come, let us deal
> wisely with them or they will multiply and in the event
> of war, they will also join themselves to those who hate
> us and fight against us and depart from the land." So they
> appointed taskmasters over them to afflict them with hard
> labor. And they built for Pharaoh storage cities, Pithom
> and Raamses. But the more they afflicted them, the more
> they multiplied and the more they spread out so that

they were in dread of the sons of Israel. The Egyptians compelled the sons of Israel to labor rigorously; and they made their lives bitter with hard labor in mortar and bricks and at all kinds of labor in the field, all their labors which they rigorously imposed on them. Then the king of Egypt spoke to the Hebrew midwives, one of whom was named Shiphrah and the other was named Puah; and he said, "When you are helping the Hebrew women to give birth and see them upon the birthstool, if it is a son, then you shall put him to death; but if it is a daughter, then she shall live." But the midwives feared God—thank the Lord for that—and did not do as the king of Egypt had commanded them, but let the boys live. So the king of Egypt called for the midwives and said to them, "Why have you done this thing, and let the boys live?" The midwives said to Pharaoh, "Because the Hebrew women are not as the Egyptian women; for they are vigorous and give birth before the midwife can get to them. So God was good to the midwives, and the people multiplied, and became very mighty. Because the midwives feared God, He established households for them. Then the Pharaoh commanded all the people, saying, "Every son who is born you are to cast him into the Nile, and every daughter you are to keep alive."

Now a man from the house of Levi went and married a daughter of Levi. The woman conceived and bore a son; and when she saw that he was beautiful, she hid him for three months. But when she could hide him no longer, she got him a wicker basket and covered it over with tar and pitch. Then she put the child into it and set it among the reeds by the bank of the Nile. Then she put the child into the basket and set it among the reeds by the bank of the Nile. His sister stood at a distance to find out what would happen to him. The daughter of Pharaoh came down to bathe at the Nile, with her maidens walking alongside the Nile; and she saw the basket among the reeds and sent her maid, and she brought it to her. When she opened it, she saw the child, and behold, the boy was crying. And she had pity on him and said, "This is one of the Hebrews' children." Then his sister said to Pharaoh's daughter, "Shall I go and call a nurse for you from the Hebrew women that she may nurse the child for you?" Pharaoh's daughter said to her, "Go ahead." So the girl went and called the child's mother. Then Pharaoh's daughter said to her, "Take this child away and nurse him for me and I will give you your wages." So the woman took the child and nursed him. The child grew, and she brought him to Pharaoh's daughter and he became her son. And she named him Moses, and said, "Because I drew him out of the water."

When most of us think of this story, we equate it to the famous movie, directed by Cecile D'Mille, *The Ten Commandments*, starring Charlton Heston as Moses and Yul Brenner as the Pharaoh. A floating basket, cascading gently down a calm, serene river, portrays the scene of Moses. As the story unfolds, we picture Pharaoh's daughter quietly bathing near the river and express a sigh of relief when she takes Moses' basket into safety. Although Hollywood has created this memorable, touching scene, as I read through the biblical account, I am reminded that the Nile was a very dangerous river. It was not a gentle, calm body of water. It was also the place where neighboring Hebrew families were filled with horror as they watched their first born sons drowned by the Pharaoh's soldiers. Quite a different picture, wouldn't you say?

Jochebed's courage is inspiring as we consider her story. As the Scriptures explain, the Hebrews were under extreme duress and treated harshly while in exile. The Egyptians afflicted the Hebrews with "harsh" tasks in an effort to keep them from being a threat to the Egyptian army. It says, "The more they afflicted the children of Israel, the stronger they grew." (The Hebrews were the children of Israel.) Through the Pharaoh's fear and intimidation of the growing Hebrew nation, he issued a decree that all Hebrew male babies were to be drowned in the Nile River. This was the Pharaoh's demented way of somehow keeping the Hebrews from advancing against his army by annihilating these innocent children.

During this extremely harsh and stressful time, Jochebed was pregnant. She obviously had no idea whether she was carrying a baby girl or boy, and no advanced ultrasounds or pregnancy tests could tell her. The time came and she delivered a healthy baby boy. The Scripture says that she "hid the child for three months." I'm not sure exactly how she hid an infant. Did he cry? Did people in the town notice that her baby bump was gone? We do not have these details, but we know that she was successful in hiding her child.

The time came when the Lord gave Jochebed wisdom in knowing that she could no longer hide her son from the Pharaoh and his army. In the plan that God unfolded to Jochebed, we read that she crafted a hand-woven basket out of reeds and covered it with tar and pitch.

In my limited imagination, I try and picture how Jochebed felt as she wove this basket. Sometimes when we read Scripture, we might be tempted to believe that courageous people, like Jochebed, were without emotion or expression when moving into arenas when supernatural faith was required. I imagine this godly woman standing at the water's edge carefully selecting reeds of the right size and weight that would be used to carry her baby safely. I also imagine as she covered the basket in tar and pitch, she checked and double-checked to make sure she adequately had covered it. I envision her arising in the morning and falling asleep at night, praying for her child's protection and for wisdom from God with the right timing to execute the plan. Releasing her baby into the Nile River had to be a heart-wrenching experience, to say the least.

The day arrived when Jochebed awoke, nursed her baby one last time, carefully swaddled him, placed him in the basket she crafted, and said her final good-bye. Don't you imagine that she doubted herself? Don't you think that she played the scenario over and again in her mind and wanted a different outcome? Do you think she struggled with fear over the crocodiles and deadly snakes that lived in the river? I'm sure she did. However, I also have to believe that God was directing her actions, reassuring her through His word, and gave her faith to trust God's plan for her and for her baby.

The story continues with the release of the basket into the Nile River. Jochebed sends her daughter, Miriam, ahead to watch closely as her baby floats down the river. As Miriam is running alongside the river, she notices the Pharaoh's daughter bathing nearby. The Pharaoh's daughter notices the little basket and calls one of her servants to go and find out what it is. Opening the basket, the servant discovers the beautiful baby boy and Pharaoh's daughter takes him to safety. The Pharaoh's daughter names him "Moses" meaning "because he is drawn from the water." Miriam, close by, is watching everything unfold. The Pharaoh's daughter calls to Miriam, recognizing her as a Hebrew. Miriam is then given the task of finding a wet nurse to care for the newfound child. Miriam excitedly runs home and volunteers her mother for the job. Jochebed is not only given her child back, safe and sound, but she is also paid wages to nurse and care for him.

I love this story for many reasons. To me, it is a beautiful portrait of God's redemptive plan perfectly executed as Jochebed trusts God and *courageously* acts in obedience to His plan. Jochebed had to release her son and trust God's wisdom and purpose.

But what's the lesson in this story for us? When we release something to the Lord, we're not releasing it into a disastrous situation. We're releasing it into the hands of the Almighty, who has a purpose and a plan.

When I was in my mid-twenties, our church was beginning a building campaign to expand space for our growing church. Our pastor was challenging us to pray about what God wanted us to give and how we wanted to be a part of the emphasis. I've always loved giving and began to pray about what the Lord wanted me to give. About two weeks before the offering was to be collected, the Lord had not spoken to me clearly regarding an amount to give for this offering. I called my pastor, and said, "Pastor Randy, what do you do if you've asked the Lord, and He hasn't given you an amount that He wants you to give?" And he said, "Well, I'll tell you what I've done in the past when that has happened to me. I go around my house and look at things and say, 'Lord, do you want this? Whatever I have belongs to You. What is it that You want?'" I thought this was a good idea, and I decided to try it. I walked around my house and began to pray. I stood by my piano and asked, "Lord, do you want my piano?" There was no answer. I moved to the den and asked, "Lord, do you want my couch?" There was no answer. Frustrated, I went back into the kitchen to continue the day's activities all the while trying to understand why I was experiencing radio silence from God.

Our music minister asked me to sing a solo for the service when the offering would be collected. Because I was fearful of forgetting words when performing a solo, I made a habit of sitting down and writing out the words to the song over and again, which helped me. As I was writing, I held the notebook with my left hand. Glancing down, I noticed my wedding ring. In my heart, I heard the Lord speak and say, "I want your ring." I sat quietly for a moment and responded, "Well, it's mine, and it's precious to me. Wouldn't you rather have the piano?" I sat quietly as I pondered this unusual request for my wedding ring. In monetary value, many other things that I owned were more valuable than my ring. In my heart, however, nothing was more precious.

The next morning I went to church prepared to sing the solo I had been assigned. When the song was completed, I slowly walked back to take my seat in the choir loft. The offering music began, and my heart began to beat faster and faster. I didn't want anyone to know that I was going to give my ring, so I quietly slipped it off under my choir robe and placed it in an offering envelope. The offering music seemed to last for hours, although I know it was only a few minutes. When the offering plate came to me, I placed my envelope containing the most precious possession I had into the plate. After I gave the envelope, I looked at my bare hand with a sense of peace in obeying God, but with sorrow over giving something that meant so much.

I visited Mom and Dad soon after giving my ring in the offering. Mom immediately noticed my bare hand and asked about my ring. I confided the incident to my parents. They wept as I shared the story, but they also understood being obedient when God requires something of value. They had mentored me in this value throughout my life. Mom excused herself and returned with a gold band. It was her mother's wedding ring she inherited. She gave it to me to wear in place of the one I had given. Years passed, and to be honest, I didn't think much more about giving my ring. It was one of those times when I felt God simply wanted my obedience and sacrifice

On my wedding anniversary five years later, I stopped at my parents' home after work to enjoy a cup of coffee. They were wonderful grandparents and enjoyed picking up the children after school. We often enjoyed coffee time together in the afternoons. I noticed an odd mood in the house that day. When I spoke to my father, he had tears in his eyes, as did my mom. I became concerned and sat down to find out why they were upset. Sitting on the edge of my seat, I was anxious to hear the reason for their tears. My father began to speak and through his tears said, "I have something for you." He took out at tiny box and presented it to me. Puzzled by this, I slowly opened the box, all the while trying to read the expressions on their faces. When I looked closely at the content of the box, I saw that it was a ring. I had a huge lump in my throat and began to cry. I exclaimed, "Oh my gosh! This looks so much like the ring I gave away five years ago." My dad placed his hand on my shoulder and said, "Stephanie, that *is* the ring you gave away five years ago!" I looked at my Dad trying to make sense of what he just said. I said, "What? How? Who?"

Mom and Dad explained that apparently when I gave my ring in the offering five years earlier, someone bought it and held on to it. Through prayer, the Lord spoke to that person's heart and instructed them to bring it over to my parents' home *that afternoon.* The person obeyed, explaining everything to my parents, and left the ring for my parents to give to me. On my wedding anniversary, five years later, the ring I thought was gone forever was returned. The person who held my ring all those years had no idea when my anniversary was, but God did.

Giving my ring does not even compare to the courage of Jochebed who gave her child. However, daughters can learn an important lesson in these stories.

So often we think that when God prompts us to release things to Him—whether people, relationships, hurts, pain—that, somehow, we are being required to release them into a the unknown. God will never ask us to release something without His perfectly executed plan already in place, and His plans are always for our good.

> God will never ask us to release something without His perfectly executed plan already in place, and His plans are always for our good.

As Psalm 33:11 (NLT) reads, "But the Lord's plans stand firm forever; his intentions can never be shaken." Psalm 25:10 (NLT) reads, "All the paths of the Lord are steadfast love and faithfulness, for those who keep his covenant and his testimonies." These two verses speak boldly of the intentional and steadfast leadership of God which we can trust with confidence.

What happens when God prompts you to release a situation, relationship, or fear, and you continue to grip control of it? It suspends the work of God in that area while He patiently waits for you to trust Him.

What if Jochebed waited until she was emotionally ready to put Moses in the basket and trust God? He would have continued to grow, learn to crawl and walk, make sounds, and blow bubbles. What if the Pharaoh's army would have walked by and seen a male toddler roaming around Jochebed's home? What do you imagine the outcome would be?

The principal of releasing is not an easy one. I, too, would love to control situations and try to make the outcome what I desire. The truth is that I don't have power to transform anything; only God does.

One of the secrets in really trusting God and releasing situations into His care is to realize that He, our Father, will oftentimes cause us to release things in order to protect us or the situation.

I spoke earlier of our daughter, Jessica, who went through an extremely difficult time with her husband's choice to divorce. Regardless of her actions and attitude to desperately save their marriage, her husband was not interested. He basically walked away and never looked back.

Even though watching her go through this devastating time broke my and George's heart, we had complete confidence that God was allowing the door to close on her marriage to protect her from future devastation in this relationship. God gave Jessica peace to release the relationship, even though it broke her heart to do so.

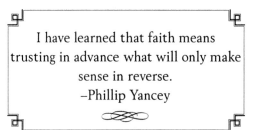

I have learned that faith means trusting in advance what will only make sense in reverse.
–Phillip Yancey

When we obediently release something that we cannot imagine living without, it doesn't mean our emotions are happy about letting it go. In fact, releasing is painful and takes time to work through the absence of the relationship or situation. However, when we metaphorically place our situation "in the basket," God's grace provides healing for our hearts, peace in the midst of the pain, and freedom.

Jochebed behaved like a daughter, not a slave. Even though God's plan for her baby had to be the most difficult to execute, *she chose to trust* and *she chose to obey* God rather than follow her natural emotions.

We, as daughters, have to also choose to trust and obey God rather than follow our own emotions when asked to surrender. Doing so is a choice and not something that will feel comfortable because it means we have to take whatever we are holding onto and let it go.

When we give situations to God, it *is* the safest place.

So, how do you give things to God? Neither the Nile River nor a reed basket is close by. Through prayer you accomplish this task. Whatever your "Moses" situation might be, releasing it to the Lord means that you spend more time in prayer than you do trying to control the situation. You get out of the way. You agree, through prayer, to trust God and take your hands off the situation. You might pray something like this:

> *Dear Father,*
> *I come to you and give you the situation regarding*
> _____. *You know my heart and know that more than anything, I want to fix this. By an act of my will, I release this situation* _____
> *to you. I trust that you are working in my behalf for good and for those whom I love. Help me trust you. Help me see your plan and trust that you are at work on behalf of this situation and will provide everything I need.*
> *In Jesus' Name*
> *Amen*

Sometimes when we are called to release our "Moses" to the Lord, we feel ill-equipped to handle the task set before us. Remember, Jochebed learned the art of working with tar and pitch during her captivity. God used the harsh tasks the Egyptians imposed to be the very skill she needed when lovingly covering her baby's basket. Although she may have also felt ill-equipped for the path God was leading, God turned a dreary daily task into the very skill that would need to provide safety for her child.

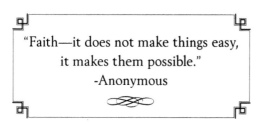

"Faith—it does not make things easy, it makes them possible."
-Anonymous

I don't know about you, but when I've had to release my own "Moses" situations, it has not been easy. My prayer time during these seasons sounds something like this: "Father, I need to know that you're working even when I cannot see it. I want to trust you, but it's hard. Forgive me for trying to manipulate what you have already taken care of. Teach me to trust even though I cannot see the result immediately. Help me not to be fearful and fill me with faith."

I may pray this same prayer a hundred times. I have had to float my heartaches down the river and trust God during many situations in my life. I cannot say that I've perfectly done this because it honestly can be quite messy moving from fear into faith. I'm so thankful for the peace of God and the patience that He gives me during these seasons.

The Hebrew word for "basket" used in this text is only used one other time in the entire Bible. The other place this same word is used is in the book of Genesis when used to describe the vessel that Noah was instructed to build. It is the word "ark." The ark was a safe place where God would also execute His plan to protect Noah and his family against disaster.

What happens when we finally put our "Moses" situation in the river and let God have it? Like Jochebed, God's plan is then executed and we watch His faithfulness in action. I'm sure that Jochebed could not have imagined how God was going to complete what He asked her to do. But God knew all along that the Pharaoh's daughter would draw out Moses from the water and raise him to be the leader He would then use to set the children of Israel free.

God's plan always trumps our imaginations.

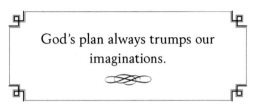

God's plan always trumps our imaginations.

Behaving as a daughter, not as a slave, in the area of courage means that we, too, will allow God to use the past in order to equip us for the future. It means that we can release our "Moses" to the Lord, knowing that God can be trusted. It also means that we exchange our fear, anxiety, and temptation to control for peace, prayer, and the reward of seeing God work.

At the end of the story, Jochebed received much more than she ever imagined. What began with a choice and obedience ended in her celebration of God's faithfulness, both in the life of her baby and in her Mother's heart as well.

Scriptures on Courage

Be strong and courageous, do not be afraid or tremble at them, for the LORD your God is the one who goes with you. He will not fail you or forsake you.

Deuteronomy 31:6(NAS)

Only be strong and very courageous, that you may observe to do according to all the law, which Moses my servant commanded you; do not turn to the right or to the left, that you may prosper wherever you go.

Joshua 1:7(NIV)

Though I walk through the valley of the shadow of death, I will fear no evil; for you are with me; your rod and your staff bring comfort to me.

Psalm 23:4(NIV)

7

THE UNFORGETTABLY FAVORED ELIZABETH AND MARY

The Unforgettably
Favored
Elizabeth and Mary

For You, O Lord, will bless the righteous; with favor.
You will surround him (her) as with a shield.

Psalm 5:12 (NKJV)

Elizabeth and Zacharias were unable to have children. Zacharias was a priest, and he was on his way to the temple to perform his priestly duties. Zacharias was surprised when his ordinary turned extraordinary by the supernatural visitation from an angel of the Lord.

Luke, 1:6–25 begins

> And an angel of the Lord appeared to him, standing to the right of the altar of incense. Zacharias was troubled when he saw the angel, and fear gripped him. But the angel said to him, "Do not be afraid, Zacharias, for your petition has been heard, and your wife Elizabeth will bear you a son, and you will give him the name John. You will have joy and gladness, and many will rejoice at his birth. For he will be great in the sight of the Lord; and he will drink no wine or liquor. And he will be filled

with the Holy Spirit—while in his mother's womb. And he will turn many of the sons of Israel back to the Lord their God. It is he who will go as a forerunner before Him in the spirit and power of Elijah, to turn the hearts of the fathers back to the children, and the disobedient to the attitude of the righteous, so as to make ready a people prepared for the Lord." Zacharias said to the angel, "How can I know this for certain?" For I am an old man and my wife is advanced in years. The angel answered him and said to him, "I am Gabriel, who stands in the presence of God, and I have been sent to speak to you and to bring you this good news. And behold, you shall be silent and unable to speak until the day when these things take place, because you did not believe my words, which will be fulfilled in their proper time." The people were waiting for Zacharias, and were wondering at his delay in the temple. But when he came out, he was unable to speak to them; and they realized that he had seen a vision in the temple; and he kept making signs to them, and remained mute. When the days of his priestly service were ended, he went back home. After these days Elizabeth his wife became pregnant, and she kept herself in seclusion for five months saying, "This is the way the Lord has dealt with me in the days when He looked with *favor* upon me, to take away my disgrace among men.

I don't imagine that either Zacharias or his wife, Elizabeth, had a clue how drastically their lives would change so quickly due to an angelic visitation. Imagine the scene—Zacharias was going about his priestly duties required in the temple. Elizabeth was probably at home, preparing dinner for the evening meal, baking bread, grinding wheat, and waiting for her husband to arrive. From the preceding Scripture, we gather that Elizabeth and Zacharias were enjoying life in their twilight years. They probably had given up on ever being parents, especially considering their age.

An angel appeared and totally rocked their world by announcing that Elizabeth would become pregnant—and pregnant with the forerunner of Christ—the Christ whom all generations had heard prophesized and who they had been waiting for. If that wasn't enough, this child would also be filled with the Holy Spirit while still in his mother's womb.

In order to understand the importance of this text, we have to realize a few important factors. This encounter happens before the birth of Jesus. The gift of the Holy Spirit was not given until after Jesus ascended to his rightful throne following his death, burial, and resurrected life. Additionally, God had chosen their child to be the forerunner—the announcer—of the coming Christ. Generations upon generations have waited for the promised Messiah. Their son would be the one to announce his presence. This was *huge* news!

Zacharias response to this news bombshell was, "How *can* I know this for certain?" In other words, he was asking how he could be sure that what he was being told would really happen. The angel, Gabriel, then reminded Zacharias that his authority came from the very throne of God. Because Zacharias questioned the authority and word from the Lord, he became mute and unable to speak until his child was born.

This consequence for Zacharias doubting what had to be shocking news may seem harsh. We certainly can understand how believing such news would be hard, right? It's important to remember that God was entrusting Zacharias and Elizabeth with something extremely important, and they needed to be confident, not wavering, as they fulfilled God's plan. After all, they had a child to raise that would radically shake up the Jewish community and the world by validating Jesus as the long-awaited Messiah.

Can you imagine what this time had to be like for Zacharias? He couldn't post his news on Facebook or Twitter because social media obviously didn't exist at the time. For that matter, there were no cell phones or land lines. Even if there were, how would he share the news? He was unable to speak! He was left only with the multitude of thoughts from the day's experience to dwell on while returning home. I can almost picture him walking through the dusty roads, trying to figure out how he was now going to be a father and how in the world he would explain everything to Elizabeth.

The story continues, and Elizabeth became pregnant with the promised child. I love Elizabeth's response to the news. She said in Luke 1:25 (NIV), "This is the way the Lord has dealt with me in the days when He looked *with favor* upon *me*, to take away my disgrace among men."

God's favor was indeed upon Elizabeth. As she embraced this amazing surprise to her destiny, she captured it with one word, "favor."

In the next chapter, another young woman also has God's favor. Her name is Mary. She was engaged to Joseph and looking forward to her new life together with her loving fiancée. Luke 1:26–45 (NIV) has her story.

> Now in the sixth month of Elizabeth's pregnancy, the angel Gabriel was sent from God to a city in Galilee called Nazareth, to a virgin engaged to a man whose name was Joseph, of the descendants of David; and the virgin's name was Mary. And coming in, he said to her, "Greetings, *favored* one! The Lord is with you." But she was very perplexed at this statement, and kept pondering what kind of salutation this was. The angel said to her, "Do not be afraid, Mary; for you have found *favor* with God. And behold, you will conceive in your womb and bear a son, and you shall name Him Jesus. He will be great and will be called the Son of the Most High; and the Lord God will give Him the throne of His father David; and He will reign over the house of Jacob forever, and His kingdom will have no end." Mary said to the angel, "How will this be, since I am a virgin?" The angel answered and

said to her, "The Holy Spirit will come upon you, and the power of the Most High will overshadow you; and for that reason the holy Child shall be called the Son of God. And behold, even your relative Elizabeth has also conceived a son in her old age; and she who was called barren is now in her sixth month. For nothing will be impossible with God." And Mary said, "Behold, the bond slave of the Lord; may it be done to me according to your word." And the angel departed from her.

Now at this time Mary arose and went in a hurry to the hill country, to a city of Judah, and entered the house of Zacharias and greeted Elizabeth. When Elizabeth heard Mary's greeting, the baby leaped in her womb; and Elizabeth was filled with the Holy Spirit. And she cried out with a loud voice and said, "Blessed are you among women, and blessed is the fruit of your womb! And how has it how has it happened to me that the mother of my Lord would come to me? For behold, when the sound of your greeting reached my ears, the baby leaped in my womb for joy. And blessed is she who believed that there would be a fulfillment of what had been spoken in her heart by the Lord.

Mary, who was engaged to Joseph, receives a very similar visitation from the angel Gabriel. However, her message was quite different for many reasons. Mary was not yet married, and she had now learned that she would have a child. Not just any child, she would have Jesus—The Messiah!

Notice Mary's response to the angel's proclamation, "How *will* this be, since I am a virgin?" Her response to Gabriel was very similar to the response Zacharias gave. However, one word makes the differences in the heart of their responses. Zacharias responded, "How *can* I know …" Mary responded, "How *will* I know?" In other words, she was not questioning whether or not this *would* happen, she was asking for wisdom in recognizing it *when* it happened. Notice also that Gabriel referred to Mary as "*favored one.*"

To me, this next section lets me know how much God "gets" us as women. Mary had just received this astounding word from the Lord. When, through the angel's news, she found out that her cousin Elizabeth already knew about this news, she ran and hurried to Elizabeth's home.

Have you ever had news—something so exciting that you are about to burst—that you could not wait to share, but at the same time, you could only share with a true, trustworthy friend? You begin going through your list of friends and family trying to decide who can be trusted with such a secret. You begin thinking, "Who can I tell this to? I have to keep it quiet! But I'm dying to share it!" Can't you just imagine Mary's mind racing as she is traveling to Elizabeth's home!

Do you imagine, like I do, that Mary ran to the door of Elizabeth's home and did not wait to knock? She just burst through the door to get to Elizabeth. Upon Elizabeth hearing Mary's voice, she rushed to her, and both women shrieked in excitement while hugging each other and weeping over God's amazing plan for their lives. As the scene unfolded, Mary touched her stomach and said, "I am giving birth to the Messiah!" Elizabeth filled with joy and excitement shared that she is giving birth to John, who would proclaim the lordship of the Messiah. I can almost imagine the exchange between these two women, whose lives were going to change, and even more so, their sons would change the world.

Elizabeth served an important role in Mary's life, both as her confidant and someone who would "amen" the Word of God. Her response to Mary's announcement is in Luke 1:42–45 (NIV): "Blessed are you among women, and blessed is the fruit of your womb! And how has it happened to me that the mother of my Lord would come to me? For behold, when the sound of your greeting reached my ears, the baby leaped in my womb for joy. And blessed is she who believed that there would be a fulfillment of what had been spoken in her heart by the Lord."

Elizabeth validates, through the Holy Spirit's wisdom in her life, the news that Mary shared. How beautiful that God would arrange for Mary to have someone like Elizabeth to believe her and stand with her as she began her journey toward mothering the Messiah.

We all need an Elizabeth in our lives. Having someone stand with us, who believes us and who encourages us as we walk out the amazing destiny God has planned for us, is important. I love that God knew that these women

We all need an Elizabeth in our lives

needed each other's faith for what would lie ahead in the lives of their sons.

I have some of the most amazing Elizabeths in my life. They love me, pray for me, laugh and cry with me, and most importantly, honestly tell me what I need to hear, even if they think I might not like what they have to say. They are the girlfriends that I share my life. They are trustworthy and godly, and precious treasures to me.

The Anti-Elizabeths

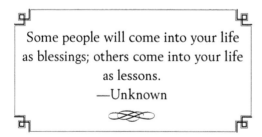
Some people will come into your life as blessings; others come into your life as lessons.
—Unknown

I've had my share of what I call "Anti-Elizabeths" as well. They are people who I once trusted and shared my life with. I was crushed later in realizing how shallow the relationship really was when I thought it grounded. Anytime we have relationships, we unfortunately will experience a mix of the good, the bad, and the ugly.

Relationships can sometimes be messy and extremely petty. We all have the potential to be "mean girls." I've been a "mean girl" a time or two in my life, and I'm not proud of it. I've had to go back to some of the people I've hurt by my own "mean girl" behavior and ask for forgiveness. I've also had to go through steps to forgive the people who have hurt me in the past in order to walk in freedom from the hurt and crushing words they shared.

When I was starting this ministry on a full-time basis, I was intimidated at what God called me to do and was so thankful to have a group of people I trusted to be partners with me. Many of them still are very precious friends. However, others, who I once considered close friends, were anything but supportive. One "Anti-Elizabeth" actually told me that she "was waiting for me to fail." To say that I was crushed at this response would be far from the truth. I was devastated.

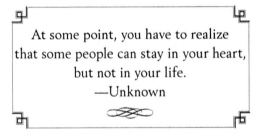

At some point, you have to realize that some people can stay in your heart, but not in your life.
—Unknown

I felt God calling me to begin a speaking ministry when I was only twenty-seven years old. I was in no way mature enough to begin speaking, but I was ready to begin the process of what God had planned for my life. That process involved studying God's Word, learning how to pray, and learning wisdom on what to share and what to withhold from sharing. I also learned the importance of allowing God to open doors in my life rather than trying to push them open in my own strength. I also learned that this ministry was not about me—it was about Him.

Many times I was *sure* that I was ready to begin speaking when I really wasn't. I finally began teaching a class that had two women participate where I could put into practice what God was teaching me. That class grew to four, then six, and as God continued to mentor me, it grew more and more. It was such a sweet time of finally stepping into the destiny God planned.

About a year after my late husband, John, went to heaven, the Lord began to speak to my heart about "walking in a manner worthy of my calling" Colossians 1:10 (NIV). I remember saying to the Lord, "Haven't I done enough hard things already? I mean, seriously?" God continued to speak, telling me to trust Him, rely on faith, and fulfill His calling in my life. Saying that I was resistant hardly expresses how I felt. After many months, I finally said, "Okay, I will trust you!" The Lord directed me to resign my job and begin the ministry full time. Let me point out at this time I had no conferences scheduled. I had nothing. But, through the months of God speaking to my heart, He ignited the fire of passion in my heart. I have to say, it was the hardest thing I felt God requiring me to do.

I spent time in prayer for wisdom, regarding the doors God promised to open. The first thing I did was establish a prayer team. God placed several friends in my heart to be part of this team. Within two days, I had a conference booking, a radio interview, and a television opportunity. I was shocked! God was not. I realized that I could trust the Lord to open doors and provide for me.

I had a vision of reaching unchurched women through hosting events and teaching on a topic relevant to women. The planned events would be fun and include sharing the gospel so they, too, could become daughters of God. Again, doors of opportunity began to open. I was still very fragile in my trust and didn't know who, if anyone would show up at these events. I often woke up during the night to plan, study, dream, and send invitations to women God was placing in my heart.

These events were unbelievably successful. Women who attended brought friends and family who did not have a personal relationship with Christ. At the end of every event, many women gave their hearts to Christ, which was very exciting. Through this season of new ministry opportunity, God continued to heal my heart and show me that life did exist after grief. Although it looked quite differently than I had planned, I was doing what I dreamed, and it was amazing. The events continued to grow and more women experienced Christ for the first time. From these events, I had the opportunity to disciple new Christians at a separate event. As the ministry grew, the word spread and the doors God opened was incredible. I was in shock, but having the time of my life.

When God has stirred something in your heart, you need an Elizabeth to believe in you. We all need those individuals who will say, "You know what? I believe in you. I'm going to stand with you and trust with you until God brings it to fruition."

We also need to all be an Elizabeth in someone else's life. Other Marys need us to stand in prayer and provide a safe place while God's plan is being worked—even if we don't completely understand it. Mary and Elizabeth both believed God to perform the impossible. They also believed the word God had given them individually.

Assignment or Affliction?

Think about the *assignment* that the Lord had given these two women. They were to be the carriers for the birth of John the Baptist and Jesus. At times God will also give an assignment to you. Maybe when you realize what God is asking you to do, you don't really like the assignment and consider it to be an affliction. You may think, "Oh Jesus, do I have to do *that?*" With dread you view your assignment.

For example, Pastor Riaan Heyns, one of our ministry leaders at New Life Church, was preaching one Sunday while Pastor Brady was out of town. Pastor Riaan said, "Jesus wants us to take Him to the darkest places because that's where He wants to be." The congregation was silent with this statement. Pastor Riaan continued, "Let me say it again: there are places that Jesus wants us to minister, to be seen, to be known, to have His glory shown, and guess what? It's our job to take Him there." It's our *assignment*. God has trusted us with this assignment. You could easily feel like what God has asked you to do is an affliction rather than His plan to share the love of Christ with those around you.

Believe me, at times, I would gladly trade assignments, if I could. I do not want to communicate that I jump for joy when given such a task. It takes moving outside of my own situation and emotions and watching what God is doing in the midst of these assignments. And, what does God want you to do for Him while moving through these seasons? Something very powerful is being in the midst of a God-assignment and being sensitive to the Holy Spirit to know what part God wants you to fulfill. God's grace, peace, and strength cover you in the midst of it.

At times the Lord will allow you to go through something because He *trusts* you to be a testimony in that moment to the people watching. And here's the deal: whatever He has trusted you with, He has already equipped you to handle.

Elizabeth and Mary "amened" each other's assignments. These daughters of God obediently and faithfully walked through this assignment. Both women had God's favor.

I love both Mary and Elizabeth's responses to the Lord's assignment. Mary said, "Let it be to me as You have said." In other words, "God, whatever you want to do in my life, I'm your girl." Elizabeth said, "I am favored by the Lord."

What if you, like Elizabeth and Mary, could walk in that favored response every day? What would change in your life? How would you walk differently? What exactly does it even mean to embrace being favored by God? Isn't that place reserved for such amazing women such as Mother Theresa, Corrie Ten Boon, or women of the kind who lived extremely sacrificial lives?

Actually, God's favor is for all of us no matter our spiritual maturity, number of Bible verses we've memorized, or how good we believe we might be. God has the supernatural ability to love us individually, uniquely, and completely. Even though our finite minds have difficulty processing this concept, His love for us and pursuit of us is *infinite*.

In the original Hebrew word for "favor," we find the definition as the following. "Grace that which affords joy, pleasure, delight, sweetness, charm, loveliness: grace of speech." (Qbible)

He has joy, pleasure, delight, sweetness, charm, loveliness, and grace in his speech that describes us. We bring the Lord joy! He is the proud parent over us. In His eyes, not only do we walk in his favor, but we are also His *favorite*! It's as if, to God, he has only one child.

Some may read this and think, "Wow, I can get away with anything, because I have God's favor!" You need to remember that God is a loving and caring Father, but He's also wise and healthy and will allow consequences to come into our lives when we are living in destruction or sin. God's house is not full of bratty, spoiled children. He is a loving Father who displays his love for us by establishing boundaries, set forth in His Word, so that we can enjoy a life without regret, shame, guilt, or condemnation.

What's the secret to understanding how to really embrace God's favor? You can partly find it in the responses from Elizabeth and Mary.

Elizabeth said, "This is the way the Lord has dealt with me in the days when He looked with favor upon me, to take away my disgrace among men." She also said, ""And blessed is she who believed that there would be a fulfillment of what had been spoken in her heart by the Lord" (Luke 1:45)(NAS). Meanwhile, Mary said, "Behold, the bond slave of the Lord; may it be done to me according to your word" (Luke 1:39) (NAS)

Gratitude, Faith, Service

Within these three powerful responses dwells the attitude of a daughter who walks in favor of the Lord.

Elizabeth, even though she experienced disgrace from her community for her barren state, expresses God's favor on her life.

87

She approaches this response to her years of barrenness from a heart of appreciation rather than bitterness for having to wait so long. This reaction describes a character of Elizabeth's heart of *gratitude*. Elizabeth, speaking to Mary about her news, expresses extreme faith. Elizabeth believes in the fulfillment of God's Word.

Mary places her life in the hands of God, and in essence says, "God, whatever you want to accomplish through my life, I will surrender to serve you."

Before you assume that Elizabeth's and Mary's lives were paved with cotton candy and rainbows, you need to remember that both their sons would be killed by those who didn't understand their calling and didn't want their message. Still, the Lord *favored* them. Yes, you can be totally in God's favor and still experience hardship. Remember, the relationship is the ultimate key, not the circumstance. God promises to remain with you and lead you through difficulty. He never said you wouldn't have hard times. It's in the times of going through hardship, in His favor, that the strength and persistence come and help you stand on His Word rather than operate through your emotions.

Doesn't this speak volumes as you journey through this life? Maybe you've encountered tremendous trials, heartache, and suffering. Maybe you've mistakenly thought that God's favor was not anywhere to be found. One of the keys in realizing God's favor is by embracing a heart of thankfulness, faith, and surrender, no matter how you feel emotionally. I don't mean a "fake it until you make it" mentality, because faking it is unauthentic. I mean a belief system, deep in your heart, that relies on a Father who would never take His eyes off you and who is constantly working on your behalf for good. The circumstances in life will present a different case. Believing the Word and nature of God rather than believing that somehow you are not worthy of His favor is your choice. This heart transformation comes from a continual relationship with Christ by knowing His Word, spending time in prayer, and seeking His perspective and wisdom in life's journey.

God's favor rested in these women's hearts, because He knew that He could trust them to carry out this divine appointment. They walked it out in God's favor.

Maybe you are wondering if God will ever come through on what He's promised. Let me encourage you that God has not forgotten the word He has spoken to your heart or forgotten how important your circumstances are. He is with you and will fulfill the word He has given. Stand and believe, out of heart of gratitude and faith, that you, daughter, are favored in God's eyes.

"And blessed is she who believed that there would be a fulfillment of what had been spoken in her heart by the Lord" (Luke 1:45) (NAS)

Scriptures on Favor

> For you, O Lord, will bless the righteous; with favor You will surround him (her) as a shield.
>
> Psalm 5:12(NIV)

> The Lord makes His face shine upon you, and be gracious to you; the Lord lifts up His countenance upon you, and gives you peace.
>
> Number 6:25–26 (NIV)

> For I know the thoughts that I think towards you, says the Lord, thoughts of peace and not of evil, to give you a future and a hope.
>
> Jeremiah 29:11 (NIV)

8

THE UNFORGETTABLY FORGIVEN, MARY MAGDALENE

THE UNFORGETTABLY *Forgiven,* MARY MAGDALENE

Forgiveness is unlocking the door to set someone free
and ... realizing *you* were the prisoner!

—Max Lucado

It was a warm summer morning, and the sun was shining bright in the city square. The children were running and playing as the women were carefully shopping at the open market to select the perfect vegetables to accompany their evening meal. The sound of laughter came from the corner of the square where the men, young and old, were gathered, sharing tales of days gone by.

Interrupting this picturesque summer's day was a sudden cloud of dust and the distant cries of a woman, obviously in trouble. The folks who were enjoying their slow summer's day suddenly had their attention drawn to the scene unfolding before their eyes. A well-known woman in the town stood half dressed and trying desperately to cover herself as a man, a Pharisee, was pulling her unwilling body into the center of the city. As their curiosity was roused, the onlookers began to gather around this dust-stormed scene. The cries of the woman grew louder and more intense. Even more vocal was the Pharisee's proclamation regarding this woman's activity.

Jesus was also in the city that day. As he was speaking with some of the people in the town, he heard one of the Pharisees, the religious leaders, address him. "Teacher, this woman has been caught in adultery, in the very act. Now in the Law Moses commanded us to stone such women; what then do You say" (John 8:3)(NIV)

Jesus, quietly but confidently, took a moment to consider the Pharisee's question. Jesus knew that the religious leaders were attempting to catch him in what they considered a variation of the law, in order to accuse him. To the surprise of the Pharisee and the other religions leaders present, Jesus stooped on the ground and began writing in the sand while the Pharisee impatiently awaited his answer.

This delay in response caused the religious leaders to only grow more impatient, so they continued to badger Jesus with the accusation at hand. Meanwhile, the woman in the center of this controversy was weeping, wailing, and begging for her life. Surrounding her now was a multitude of her neighbors, all waiting for the answer from Jesus. She knew it would be only moments before she realized the consequences of her act of adultery—stoning. Crouching down in order to somehow shield herself from the impending stoning, she whimpered as she awaited her punishment.

Jesus slowly rose and spoke to the crowd. The people were holding their breath, waiting for the answer to the consequences of this woman's sin. The men and women were horrified, but they also were feeling a righteous judgment for the woman with the reputation. While awaiting Jesus' response, the people began to gather their stones for the moment of truth. The religious leaders were staunchly standing, with their arms folded as they waited for what they considered to be an easy answer. Jesus looked intently into the eyes of the crowd and said, "He, who is without sin among you, let him be the first to throw a stone at her" (John 8:7) (NIV).

This response was met with silence. Jesus then stooped back toward the ground, and again began writing in the sand with his finger. The only noise to be heard was that of the frightened, whimpering woman in the center of this chaotic scene. As she contemplated the response of Jesus, she wondered if she heard correctly. In her heart, she thought, "What does that mean? When will they begin the stoning?"

She then heard a very strange sound, "Thump, thump, thump" as the stones began to fall to the ground, one by one, followed by the footsteps of the crowd as they left the scene. Her mind was racing wildly as she considered the possibilities of what may happen next! "Will they kill me? Why are they leaving? Are they going to get others to stone me? Will I go to prison?" While she contemplated all the possibilities, she remained crouched on the ground, afraid to move.

She suddenly heard a set of footsteps moving closer to her. In her terror, she expected violence, but the gentle hand of Jesus touched her on the back, and He too crouched to the ground to speak to her. Taking his hand, He lifted her head until her tear-stained eyes met His. He took her by the hand and helped her stand. After several minutes, she attempted to compose herself all the while trying to make sense of Jesus' response. Jesus then said, "Woman, where are they? Did no one condemn you" (John 8:10) (NIV)

Through her blurry vision she looked to the right, looked to the left, and even looked behind her. She was astonished to find no one left from the mob ready to take her life. She shook her head, almost in disbelief, and said, "No one, Lord." Jesus responded and said to her, "I do not condemn you either. Go. From now on, sin no more" (John 8:11) (NIV).

She began to assemble her torn clothes in order to cover the bareness of her shoulders while gazing in Jesus' eyes. She desperately was trying to comprehend what had just taken place. Something inside of her felt strangely different—a feeling she has never experienced before and so much more than relief from impending death. She began to feel a sense of peace and wholeness. Still not sure exactly what happened to her, she gratefully left her life of sin, and for the first time, she realized that she has been given a brand new life.

This account of Mary Magdalene, as found in John, Chapter 8, is a beautiful portrayal of the power of forgiveness. Jesus knew Mary's sin, and He also knew the law, for which the Pharisees were waiting for Jesus to break. He didn't break any laws; he simply asked a question that dissolved the religious leaders attempt to trick him and set Mary Magdalene free.

Notice that Jesus didn't validate the sin. He did not excuse her behavior or say that she had not sinned. He knew, in fact, that the allegations were correct. He gave her grace, forgave her, and instructed her to live a different life.

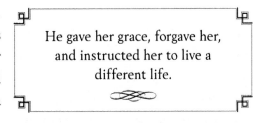

He gave her grace, forgave her, and instructed her to live a different life.

The power of forgiveness is typically much underrated. If we truly understood its value, we would be quicker to offer it and wiser to accept it as well. Maybe the reason we sometimes delay the power of forgiveness is because we don't truly understand it.

In order to understand what forgiveness *is*, we first have to understand what it is *not*.

Forgiveness Is Not …

Forgiveness is not saying that sin is okay. Sometimes people confuse forgiveness with agreement in sin. Sin has consequences. Period. Forgiveness does not negate the consequences of sin.

As a child, my mom would take me to our neighborhood grocery store. I loved going with her because the store had a large assortment of candy. On one of our visits, I noticed a particularly attractive offering in the candy section—purple, edible wax fingernails. These delightful candy-shaped nails intrigued me, and I asked if I could have some. She took a moment to consider my question and said, "Not this time, Stephanie." In our home, you only asked once. When you received a "no" answer, you dropped the subject. I didn't appreciate the fact that she didn't see the same value in the edible wax fingernails as I did, so I decided that my need for these was greater than her reason for not having them. I quietly grabbed a handful of the candied nails and went around the corner of the aisle, out of my mother's sight. I had to be quick, because she was like an eagle and could spot you miles and miles away. I quickly shoved the candied nails into my pockets while Mom was distracted paying her bill.

The drive home seemed like an eternity, although it was probably only ten minutes. I was consumed with devising a plan to convince my mother that somehow, these candied nails followed me home and magically appeared. I pictured the scene playing out well where Mom would also be amazed at the candy's appearance and joyfully watch as I wore my new purple wax fingernails with pride.

While Mother was unloading our groceries, I jumped out of the car and quickly reached for the candied nails. In my panicked state, trying not to be caught, I took the nails and threw them all over the ground in front of me. When my mother came around the side of the car where I was standing, I exclaimed, "Mom! Look! It's like magic! The purple wax fingernails are here! The same ones I wanted at the grocery!"

The expression on my mother's face let me know that this scene was not going to play out as I imagined. Mom and I did not share any joyous celebration that day. She instead steadily put the groceries down and scowled at my poor attempt to hide my sin. Like any good mother, she picked me up, placed me back in the car along with my purple candy wax fingernails, and began driving. I knew better than to try to explain, so I simply asked, "Where are we going?" She responded, "Right back to the grocery store so you can explain to Mr. Holmes why you chose to steal from his store." I was mortified. Mr. Holmes was a kind, gentle man who would always shared items from the deli located in the back of his store with me. I was so ashamed and dreaded the thought of telling him what I had done.

Mom firmly grabbed my hand as we walked back into the grocery store. She paraded me in front of the other customers and said, "Mr. Holmes, Stephanie has something she would like to say to you." I stood there and began to cry. Mom spoke up and said, "Stephanie, what do you have to say to Mr. Holmes?" I quietly whispered, "Mr. Holmes, I am very sorry because I stole these purple candy wax fingernails and did not pay for them." Mr. Holmes looked pathetically at me and said, "It's okay this time, Stephanie, but please do not ever do that again." He gave me a gentle little hug, and Mom escorted me right back to my home and into my room where I spent the larger part of my day. Mr. Holmes and my mother forgave me, and I learned a very valuable lesson about the consequences of stealing.

Sin has consequences. Forgiveness does not let those who sin off the hook regarding the consequences. God holds the account of sin and will handle appropriately when others harm or seek to destroy.

Forgiveness Is a Choice, Not a Feeling ...

The thought of forgiveness is not something that you will immediately feel when you've been wronged. Quite the contrary. You will feel like getting revenge, wanting the other person to pay to self-gratify the hurt you've experienced. If you wait until you feel like forgiving, that day may never arrive. Forgiveness is something you do as an act of your will, whether you feel like it or not because you want to obey God's Word and live a life without regret.

Forgiveness Is Not for Other's Benefit As Much As It Is for Yours ...

When you choose to hold on to hurt, resentment, anger, and hatred because of the sin of others, you actually are allowing the offender to have power over you. How so? When you operate out of these emotions, you allow yourself to replay over and again the offense, sometimes to the fullest detail. Through this ongoing repeat of the past, you give your emotional, spiritual, and physical attention to the actions of others rather than focusing on your future. Doing so paves a crooked path for remaining in the past and becoming a resentful, stuck person. And typically, the offender has moved past the incident and on to better things. If the offender were as concerned as you are with their offense, he or she would have already sought reconciliation. You become a subject of his or her behavior and then trapped by it instead of set free from it.

God Will Heal Your Hurt When You Choose to Forgive ...

God desires to heal you from the hurts of others. When you, through an act of your will, release the offense and choose to pick up a heart of forgiveness, God then is able to heal the places where your emotions have been damaged by the sin of others. Repeatedly replaying the offense forces the hurt to fester and makes healing impossible.

Mary Magdalene needed forgiveness. Her lifestyle was destructive both to her and to the men she entertained. Her sin kept her from realizing her value as a woman and as a daughter of God. She became comfortable in her cheapened lifestyle and began to accept it as her identity. Jesus spoke to the core of her heart when he said, "Woman, where are your accusers?" Perhaps Jesus was speaking not only to the crowd that surrounded her with stones, but also to the many people who mocked and ridiculed her life of sin. Isn't it true that when Jesus speaks that He addresses the core of your heart, oftentimes the secret places that you hurt that you think no one else knows anything about?

Forgiveness Can Be a Process ...

My life has had situations where forgiveness was easier and some other situations when it required a process. I have struggled in the past to forgive some hurtful scenarios. Forgiving is not easy, but I've always been so thankful after I've experienced the freedom that comes from forgiving.

Forgiveness Is As Specific As the Layers of Hurt Received...

Through prayer, sometimes I have asked God to help me forgive. I pray through the situation, and as an act of my will, speak forgiveness. I usually arise from my prayer time feeling released and much better, until I remember the hurt all over again. With that reminder, whether through the thoughts from the enemy, through a repeat offense that mirrors the hurt I'm working through, or through the person continuing to be careless in the relationship, I once again experience the flood of emotions associated with the hurt. Again, I spend time in prayer and ask God to help me forgive the hurt and lay down any resentment I am harboring.

Remembering that God made you a spiritual, physical, and emotional being is important. You are not a robot. Depending on the amount of harm you have experienced determines the length of time it takes for God to heal your damaged emotions and give you the ability to lay down the offense once and for all.

You may think that if you share your hurt and offense more than once to God that you didn't actually forgive in the first place. That's not always true, especially when the hurt runs deep. God continues to uncover areas that need to be healed, thus making forgiveness a process alongside your healing. He knows when you are ready.

What If You Are the One Who Needs Forgiveness ...

If you need forgiveness from others, seeking reconciliation as soon as possible is critical. Depending on the nature how you've offended will determine whether you can or should salvage the relationship. As Romans 12:18 (NIV) says, "If it is possible, as far as it depends on you, live at peace with everyone."

For example, consider Mary Magdalene's offense. Not only did she need to receive forgiveness for her life of sin, she also needed to seek forgiveness from the people she hurt *through* her sin. Scripture doesn't give us details regarding her process of forgiveness, but we can look at Scripture and find the appropriate steps.

1) **Pray and seek wisdom from the Lord as to how, when, and what you should do to seek forgiveness.** I can't press enough the importance of this step. Out of your guilt for what you've done, you may want to run immediately and try to rectify the situation. Sometimes you need to do so; sometimes doing so can actually be more destructive. We need the Lord's wisdom and the counsel of others.

2) **Refuse the temptation to share the offense with multitudes of people in order to make you feel better about the offense.** As you work through the process, again ask the Lord and one, maybe two close friends, who have exhibited wisdom in the past. When I feel badly, I want others around me to make me feel better. If you think about it, it's actually a pretty selfish thing to do. Think about the person you've offended and whether or not he or she would appreciate your side of the story being shared without the opportunity for fair input.

As a side note to married women, please do *not* share private details of your marriage with your group of girlfriends. I can't tell you the countless times I have overheard women sharing very private relationship issues within their marriage with other people—and in public! If you are experiencing issues of forgiveness within your marriage, please only share in confidence with trusted friends or within the walls of a good counseling center. Although talking about the issue with a hundred of your closest friends or posting inappropriate remarks on social media may make you feel better, it will destroy any trust that is left within your relationship.

3) **You have many ways to seek forgiveness if one-on-one appointments aren't the best option.** If the situation is volatile, writing a letter is a good way to share your repentant heart and allow the other person to hear you without fueling a back-and-forth dispute. Again, seek the wisdom of the Lord and others for the letter's content and whether or not writing a letter is a good idea for your situation and the timing.

Take responsibility for the hurt you've caused. Own it! If you've done something to hurt another, simply take responsibility without creating a finger-pointing side to the situation. Don't say or write something, such as, "I'm really sorry that I hurt you by my actions. They were clearly wrong, but, if you wouldn't have provoked me, I would never have responded the way I did." This response is not taking responsibility. This response is making the other person responsible for your behavior. Regardless of what other people do, you are only responsible for *your* actions. Having a repentant heart and sincerely apologizing for hurt is the first step in reconciling relationships.

> Apologizing—Does not always mean you are wrong and the other person is right. It just means you value your relationship more than your ego.
> —Anonymous

Forgiveness Is the Tool by Which You Are Set Free ...

Mary Magdalene walked away a different woman that day. To some people, she may have appeared the same on the outside, but inside her heart she experienced a new life, a new beginning that she may have never thought possible. She was set free from her life of sin, years of condemnation, guilt, and pain, and she discovered that her value could come from something other than another woman's husband. She experienced, in full, God's amazing power of forgiveness.

How do we know for sure that Mary's heart was changed that day? How do we know that she truly grasped the forgiveness she received? We can find the answer to this question in John 20:1–18 (NIV). The setting for this story was in a graveyard. Jesus had been cruelly crucified and buried in a friend's tomb. It was three days following Jesus' death.

> Now on the first day of the week Mary Magdalene came early to the tomb, while it was still dark, and saw the stone already taken away from the tomb. So she ran and came to Simon Peter and to the other disciple whom Jesus loved, and said to them, "They have taken away the Lord out of the tomb, and we do not know where they have laid Him." So Peter and the other disciple went forth, and they were going to the tomb. The two were running together; and the other disciple ran ahead faster than Peter and came to the tomb first; and stooping and looking in, he saw the linen wrappings lying there; but he did not go in. And so Simon Peter also came, following him, and entered the tomb; and he saw the linen wrappings lying there, and the face-cloth which had been on His head, not lying with the linen wrappings, but rolled up in a place by itself. So the other disciple who had first come to the tomb then also entered, and he saw and believed. For as yet they did not understand the Scripture that He must rise again from

the dead. So the disciples went away again to their own homes.

But Mary was standing outside the tomb weeping; and so, as she wept, she stooped and looked into the tomb; and she saw two angels in white sitting, one at the head and one at the feet, where the body of Jesus had been lying. And they said to her, "Woman, why are you weeping?" She said to them, "Because they have taken away my Lord, and I do not know where they have laid Him." When she had said this, she turned around and saw Jesus standing there, and did not know that it was Jesus. Jesus said to her, "Woman, why are you weeping? Whom are you seeking?" Supposing Him to be the gardener, she said to Him, "Sir, if you have carried Him away, tell me where you have laid Him, and I will take Him away." Jesus said to her, "Mary!" She turned and said to Him in Hebrew, "Rabboni!" [Teacher]. Jesus said to her, "Stop clinging to Me, for I have not yet ascended to the Father; but go to My brethren and say to them, 'I ascend to My Father and your Father, and My God and your God.'" Mary Magdalene came, announcing to the disciples, "I have seen the Lord," and that He had said these things to her.

You can find the fruit of Mary Magdalene's forgiven life in this text. After Jesus was crucified and then buried, where is Mary Magdalene? She is standing at the entrance of the tomb waiting. She understandably is grieved, because, along with the other disciples, she watched Jesus' horrific death.

With the absence of Jesus, she did not choose to return to her former lifestyle. Remember, the concept of someone rising from the dead was not an everyday occurrence. Jesus was careful to tell those individuals close to him over and again that after three days, He would return. Here, Mary Magdalene was waiting for Jesus.

I love the exchange between Mary and Jesus when they are conversing in the garden. Mary was so grief stricken that she didn't even recognize Jesus. The only concern she had was where Jesus could be found.

The woman who was once a picture of disgrace and dishonor is now the first one that speaks to Jesus after his resurrection. Mary's life had indeed changed. Her heart, filled with the overwhelming gratitude of forgiveness, remains faithful to follow Jesus. He honors her by giving her the task of telling the other disciples that He had indeed risen from the dead, just like He said.

What an amazing portrait of grace and forgiveness. From the moment Mary Magdalene chose forgiveness and a new life, Jesus did not look at her as a sinful woman from that unforgettable day in the city square any longer. He looked through her past and into the woman she had now become.

That is the gift of forgiveness. It supernaturally erases our failures and gives a fresh start to our lives. Only God can view us without our baggage and truly see the potential we have and the life we are meant to lead regardless of how we mess it up.

> That is the gift of forgiveness. It supernaturally erases our failures and gives a fresh start to our lives.

And, this gift of forgiveness is available for you also. You also have the opportunity to live a life of honor rather than of shame, guilt, condemnation, or destruction. Through the enormous price Jesus paid for your sin, by dying on the cross, this forgiveness is available to His daughters. Even though forgiveness is a simple process, it cost Jesus everything.

How do you live a life free from your past and free from your failures and disappointments? How do you really forgive those who have hurt you? You can find the secret in this story of Mary Magdalene. She waited for Jesus. She pressed through her past and chose to accept God's miraculous power in her life, which happened through her relationship with Jesus.

Many times I have felt such shame and guilt over sin. I have done and said things that I have deeply regretted. When I think of bringing my regrets before the Lord, I almost don't want to talk about it because I have been so ashamed. Instead I have chosen to hold onto it a little longer and try to do good things to make up for my mistakes (which is the slave mentality I discuss in chapter 2). Somehow I fool myself by thinking that God doesn't know what I've done, and, if I do enough good things, then it will equalize my regret.

As more time passes, I become more comfortable in self-deceit and continue to do good things with my slave mentality. Functioning without grace definitely lacks peace. This lack of peace robs my joy and the shame of my actions causes me then to have a minimal prayer life and Bible study. Before long, I feel quite miserable.

God always knows where to find me. I can diminish my prayer time and Bible study, and I can do all the good things that make me temporarily feel better, but He pursues me. He is relentless in His pursuit to bring me back into a right relationship with Him—not to scold and punish me, but because I am His daughter and He delights in me. My Father is grieved to see me miserable and is ready to provide the

> He is relentless in His pursuit to bring me back into a right relationship with Him—not to scold and punish me, but because I am His daughter and He delights in me.

forgiveness I need in order to set me free. When I finally give in and bring my regrets before the Lord through prayer, He heals me and sets me free.

When my oldest daughter, Jessica, was 2½ years old, we were spending time together while I completed my daily chores. At the time, John Mark was 18 months old and napping. Keeping Jessica busy so John Mark could take a nap was always a good idea. She was always my little helper, and she loved helping with just about everything and would cheerfully exclaim, "I do it, Mommy ... by myself."

One afternoon we were working around our home and I heard this interesting sound. I walked closer to the sound and recognized it to be cellophane being opened. I was curious to see what Jessica was up to, so I stood and just listened. "Crunch, crunch, crunch," the cellophane noise continued as I spotted little Miss Jessica in our pantry. I knew there was nothing of danger in the pantry, so I continued to stand where she could not see me and just observe.

After several minutes of the cellophane crunching, I heard the pantry door close ever so quietly. I then saw my sweet little angelic daughter tiptoeing out of the kitchen. As she rounded the corner where I was standing, I said, "Jessica, what have you been doing?" Astonished, she looks up at me, placed her hands innocently in the air, and said, "I not doing nothing, Mommy!" What she didn't realize is that her face was *covered* in chocolate! I was trying not to laugh, so I said, "Are you sure?" Jessica replied, while shaking her head prominently, "Nooooooo, Mommy!"

This moment was honestly the first time I had witnessed my little angel not tell the truth and then insist that somehow I was mistaken. I leaned down to make eye contact with this little, chocolate-covered face and say, "Jessica, you can tell Mommy what you were doing. I want you to tell the truth." Jessica then put her head down to look at the floor and quietly said, "Mommy, I was not doing nothing."

I took her by the hand and brought her to the bathroom counter. I picked up my little girl and stood her on the counter so she could see her chocolate-covered face. When she looked into the mirror and saw the multitude of chocolate around her mouth, nose, and cheeks, she looked at me and said, "Mommy, I dirty." I began to wipe off her face while she apologized for not telling the truth. We talked about the importance of obeying while continuing to clean her up her chocolate mess. Moments later, we hugged, and she was back to enjoying her busy time with me.

This simple picture represents God's heart of forgiveness for us. We delay the process because we are not sure God can really love us unconditionally. We understand His love when our performance is spot on, and we are mystified by His love when we don't deserve it. This is the true heart of our Father. He sees our chocolate-covered faces and is more concerned with our relationship than our failures. He waits to wipe off the mess, forgive us, hug us, and set us back on the path where we once again have peace.

I sometimes think that forgiving me, by letting go of my failures, is so much harder than forgiving others.

In my very early twenties, I was a hot mess. I suffered from an eating disorder from the time I was sixteen years old. My college roommate and I shared the obsession with being thin. I was five-feet tall and weighed around 93 pounds in college. My roommate was a little taller, but equally as thin. We found a doctor who would prescribe diet pills for us, and we then learned the art of addiction. I began experimenting with pills, diet pills, fluid pills—just about anything I could get my hands on that would reduce the numbers on the bathroom scale. When I did eat, because I was starving myself, I then forced myself to throw everything up, which resulted in me being addicted to bulimic behavior.

Because I was taking diet pills with energizers, I would stay up all night, although I was not able to concentrate. My roommate and I would clean our rooms or go outside to run rather than sleep. After a while, this behavior began to take its toll and I began missing class. I was a vocal music education major and went from being a featured soloist to a regular member of the choir because of the downward spiral I found myself in. I became further and further behind in my studies and had to drop several classes and receive an incomplete.

I went home for Thanksgiving break and announced to my parents that I would be taking a semester off because I wanted to work. Over the Thanksgiving holiday, I found a job that paid well and was something I enjoyed. I went back to college and announced to my professors that I would be taking a sabbatical from my studies.

I began my new job and my new boss seemed to really like me. I was twenty-one years old and extremely naïve. The boss and I went to meetings out of the office together, which at first felt really awkward, but as time continued, felt more normal. I loved my new job, I loved being out of college, and I thought I had the world in my hands.

My boss and I spent lots of time together in and out of meetings and sometimes even staying late to complete projects after work. My mom began to notice a change in me and said, "Stephanie, be careful with your boss." I thought that was an odd thing to say and responded, "Mom, of course!"

As weeks continued, the work relationship with my boss changed. I noticed him staring at me during meetings. In the mornings, I found little notes that he had written for me the night before. We went to lunch together and continued spending much time together in between our meetings.

I developed feelings for him, and what once would have seemed so creepy, began to feel more accepting. However, my newly found feelings had two problems: he was twenty-five years older, and he was married.

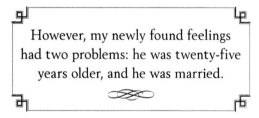

However, my newly found feelings had two problems: he was twenty-five years older, and he was married.

I knew this behavior was wrong, but I felt like a part of me was alive. My life had continued its downward spiral with the eating disorder in full force. The addiction was my best friend, and I now crossed a line by entertaining a relationship with a married man.

God found me in the midst of my mess and relentlessly pursued me all the while I was part of this destructive pattern. When I turned my heart to the Lord rather than follow the destructive path

I was on, I came to my senses through God's forgiving power. I quit my job and apologized to my boss for my behavior and returned to the peace-filled life I previously had.

It took a while to heal my heart, regarding my sin. I had known better, and I was so ashamed on so many levels. With sin comes its consequences, and for me, they were many. It was hard. A large part of me felt so dirty that I had huge temptation just to continue in sin. After all, I had already blown it, but a larger part of me knew that God had a destiny for me that was much greater than any mess I was in. God's healing continued, and I am so thankful for the new life that God provided despite of my horrible choices.

Isn't it true that when secrets involving shame and guilt are captured in our heart, it is a miserable time, indeed? These thoughts and accusations from our past can continue to pop in our minds at the most random times. These thoughts come from the enemy whose main purpose is to render us ineffective by continuing to dwell on the past. When those areas are left to grow, take root, and bloom within us, we can begin to operate out of our failure rather than out of our strengths.

How does this destructive progression happen? When these inner feelings of unworthiness or insecurity from our past dwell, we can find ourselves making compromised choices outside of God's best for us. These compromised choices will affect our relationships, the people we choose to surround

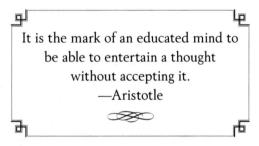

It is the mark of an educated mind to be able to entertain a thought without accepting it.
—Aristotle

ourselves, and our self-image, and they can even keep us from trusting others simply because we don't think we deserve the best.

I don't imagine that Mary Magdalene started her life with the goal of being known as "the sinful woman." Something must have happened that caused her to direct her life by shame and guilt rather than freedom and peace. No matter what events previously took place in her life or how she arrived at her stage of life, Jesus settled the score by forgiving her and asking, "Where are your accusers?"

That's a powerful question that we can apply to our lives today. If we have sought forgiveness or to be forgiven but continue to live with the guilt and shame, we should ask ourselves, "Where are our accusers?" In other words, who is doing the condemning? Is it other people or do we condemn ourselves? Today can be the day to settle this issue. If something has harbored in your heart either from the hurt from others or your own self-inflicted pain, ask Jesus to forgive and give you a brand new life and outlook. Ask Jesus to show you how *He* sees you and accept his grace, mercy, and clean slate. And, just as Jesus instructed Mary Magdalene, go, and don't return to the past. Walk confidently, as His daughter, into the destiny God has planned for you.

Scriptures on Forgiveness

> Come now, let us reason together, says the Lord; though your sins be as scarlet, they shall be as white as snow; though they are red like crimson, they shall become as wool.
>
> Isaiah 1:18(NIV)

> Come to me, all who labor and are heavy laden, and I will give you rest. Take my yoke upon you and learn from me, for I am gentle and lowly in heart, and you will find rest for your souls. For my yoke is easy and my burden is light.
>
> Matthew 11:28–30(NIV)

> Love is patient and kind; love does not envy or boast; it is not arrogant or rude. It does not insist on its own way; it is

not irritable or resentful; it does not rejoice in wrongdoing, but rejoices with the truth. Love bears all things, believes all things, hopes all things, and endures all things.

1 Corinthians 13:4–7(NIV)

9

THE UNFORGETTABLE DESTINY
OF A PRINCESS

THE UNFORGETTABLE *Destiny* OF A PRINCESS

So this is love. So this is what makes life divine.

—Cinderella

I have two adorable nieces, Alicia and Tatiana, who are six and three years old. They are the daughters of my younger brother, Steven and his sweet wife, Jung. Steven is eight years younger than I, and so George and I have enjoyed his children more like our "pretend" grandchildren rather than nieces.

Alicia and Tatiana are very much girly girls. Alicia's favorite color is purple, and Tatiana's favorite color is pink. We especially love when they come to visit because our children are now adults. Our household is filled with an extra measure of excitement and joy when Alicia and Tatiana are here.

Before they visit, we always go to the shopping center and select a variety of princess items for each girl. We take all the items we've purchased and hide them in our bedroom. Every morning when our little rays of sunshine awake, we have a special princess present for the day, ranging from coloring books, puzzles, dress-up items, or princess snacks. They wear their tiaras for breakfast, lunch, and dinner, and they make sure the day includes lots of princess activities complete with the right amount of "bling" fit only for a *real* princess. It is a celebration to say the least! Making memories with my little nieces also brings back such sweet memories of my childhood love for princesses.

When I grew up, the little girls in my neighborhood played a regular game of "rescue the princess." Because we grew up in the late 1960s, one of the popular children's hairstyles at that time was a pixie haircut— a very short hairstyle—not anywhere as fashionable as Halle Berry. None of us had the long, flowing hair that was a must for any princess. We solved this problem by taking our sweaters, placing the collar of the sweater around our faces, and buttoning the sweaters up, which made the collar fit perfectly around our faces. In a matter of seconds, we had long flowing sweater-hair that cascaded as we would swing on the swing set. Our sweater-hair came in a variety of textures and colors from white to pink and even red. We often forced one of our little brothers to play with us; after all, every princess needs a Prince Charming.

I loved reading the popular princess stories, such as Snow White, Sleeping Beauty, and my favorite, Cinderella, just to name a few. In each story of these young women, a daughter to a king enjoys a happy childhood filled with everything life can offer. Although their journey begins well, an evil force, jealous of their position, disrupts and seeks to harm. Each story has the balance of good and evil—and good always prevails. After all, these stories have to finish with the popular scene where the princess and her charming prince ride together into the sunset, happily ever after.

Destiny of a Princess

The Disney movies beautifully portray the destinies of their princesses typically being rescued from harm by a kind, and often handsome, prince. Our hearts may skip a beat while watching the damsel, who was once in distress; be courageously rescued from harm by the man of her dreams.

As we are well aware, life is not a Disney movie. I don't know about you, but my days do not begin by opening my windows to lovely chirping birds, fluttering butterflies, and singing animals, as well as a fairy godmother who is ready to begin sewing beautiful clothes for me while she completes all the housework.

Although Walt Disney has done an incredible job of giving us a fantasy impression of the princess lifestyle, it does not compare with the destiny that God has planned for each of us. God's fulfillment in our life brings valuable attributes far more precious than Disney could ever portray. Proverbs 31:25 (MSG) "She is clothed in strength and dignity and she laughs without fear of the future.

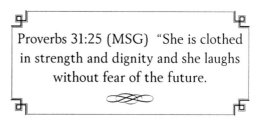

Proverbs 31:25 (MSG) "She is clothed in strength and dignity and she laughs without fear of the future.

We Have a Destiny ...

God has planned a unique destiny for each of us to fulfill. Our destinies are as unique as our personalities. Each one is custom-designed to complement our temperament, personality, heart, and passion. No two destinies are alike.

My husband George is a business consultant. He travels and meets with business leaders to bring about change that will better serve the people in their company, help them operate more effectively, and make improvements to save sometimes millions of dollars. He operates his business out of a supernatural gift from the Lord. George has said repeatedly that he believes his destiny includes "influencing influencers," much like the biblical destinies of Daniel or Joseph.

I shared earlier that my destiny involves a conference ministry. I pray and ask God for a specific word for women, teach the Word of God, and have the privilege of seeing the transformation power of the Holy Spirit. I, too, operate out of a supernatural gift from the Lord to fulfill God's destiny for me.

Our destinies are quite different, just as we are. George is an intellectual person who inwardly processes, thinks in linear lines, and has a gift of seeing far into the future with a big-picture approach to life. I am a person who outwardly processes, thinks in a mosaic style (several thoughts within the same conversation), and am more detailed in my approach to life. Both George and my destiny are equally important because we are fulfilling what God has purposed our lives to represent while here on the earth.

Your destiny may not include being a business consultant or a conference speaker, but God has selected a special plan for only *you* to fulfill, and it matters. At times you may get stuck along the way and lose your heart and passion for the plan God has ordained for your life.

I teach a weekend women's conference on the topic of destiny titled, "The Stiletto Project—Stepping into Your Destiny." Together we discover God's plan for our lives and really embrace the destiny God has in mind. Needless to say, it is a powerful weekend! I get so excited to hear stories of women, who prior to the conference, had no idea what they were supposed to accomplish come to realize God's amazing plan for their lives.

Through the weekend, it's not unusual for some women to sort of hit a wall in coming to grips with feelings of being forgotten, unworthy, or bitter about the cards in life they've been dealt. Recognizing areas that are unhealed by the Lord is a huge part in overcoming the forgotten attitude toward God. Overcoming the forgotten attitude toward God is also extremely important in order to truly trust God's plan for the future. Sometimes our journey isn't what we want or imagine. We have to work through feelings of disappointment or resentment before we can truly embrace the truth that God intends to use the mess for good.

I once met a woman at one of the "Stiletto Project" conferences who had such an issue. After I completed teaching one of the sessions, she approached me. She walked swiftly toward me with her arms folded across her chest and a scowl planted on her face. As I saw her approach, I thought, "Oh no. This may not be good." She stood in front of me, leaned into my face, and barked out these words, "And *what* do you do when God doesn't care about you?" I was quiet. She remained in her aggressive stance, almost glaring as if she dared me to provide the wrong answer. I remained quiet. One of the more valuable things God has taught me is to know when to be quiet and know when to speak. I internally was praying and asking the Holy Spirit for wisdom. The Lord spoke in my heart and said, "Ask her about her husband." I looked at her and said, "Tell me about your husband." When I spoke those words, she began flailing her arms in the air as she exclaimed, "Well, I'm glad you asked! We just married six months ago, and now he is sick and I am so angry because of his health conditions!" I tried to keep a poker face with this response, but I believe my jaw hit the floor with this news. The question only fueled the forest fire, blazing within her. I again internally prayed and waited for God to give me wisdom and again, and I was quiet. She resumed her folded-arm position while she waited for my response. The Lord spoke again and said, "Ask her about her husband again, but this time ask her about her *first* husband." As I pondered for a second what was about to come out of my mouth, I purposefully took a step back, just in case. I said, "Okay, thank you for sharing that, but tell me about your *first* husband." Her face fell and her arms dropped limply beside her body. As her eyes welled with tears, she said, "My *first* husband was a pastor, and he left me for another woman. My children and I were devastated and became the item of gossip around our small town; we had to relocate in order to escape condemnation." As I listened to her story, the Lord said to me, "That's where she feels forgotten and she is angry with Me." Indeed.

I did something I've never done before. I excused myself for a moment and went to get a full box of tissues, a pen, and a journal. I walked back to our conversation with my supplies in hand. She had a puzzled look on her face. I said her to her, "I have an assignment for you. I want you to take this box of tissues, journal, and pen, and go find a place of solitude within the retreat grounds. I want you to tell God everything you feel in your heart toward your first and your second marriage. And, I want you to tell God how you feel toward Him because of all this pain. If you have to scream, then scream! If you have to cry and wail, then by all means, lie on the ground and get it out! You, my friend, are filled with such anger that you can't accept anything good that God has for you, which is understandable considering the extreme loss you've faced. However this destructive force within you is preventing you from moving forward in God's healing in your life. God can handle your anger, trust me. After you've gotten everything off your chest, *wait for God to speak.* He has a word for you. Whatever God says, write it down in your journal because you will want to remember this moment. Do not come back to the conference room until you've done this." She slowly nodded her head and said, "Okay, I will try this." I prayed for her to have strength and courage during her time in the woods. I prayed that she would have a breakthrough from the anger and resentment she harbored. She left the conference room for her appointment with God.

Several hours later, we were beginning our nightly session. I was doing my usual preparation to teach, and a woman approached me with the most radiant smile and presence. I said, "Hi, how are you enjoying the weekend?" The woman looked at me and said, "Stephanie, it's me! I'm back from the woods! I did what you said!" Well, you could have knocked me over with a feather! I did not even recognize her as the same woman from the earlier encounter. Her countenance was sweet, her stance was peaceful, and her smile lit up the room. I was shocked! I said, "Tell me about your time." She shared about her experience in the woods and how, for the first time, she really told God how she felt, and God was, of course, faithful to give her a word and heal her heart. She was then ready to move into embracing God's destiny for her life. For the first time, she realized how God intended to use all the hurt and pain from the past for her good and His glory.

Since this experience, I've sent many women "into the woods," complete with their box of tissues, journal, and pen. I've also spent my own time "in the woods" with God as well. What I've learned is that it's okay to hit the wall as long as we deal with our frustration appropriately and allow God to speak truth in our lives. Waiting for God to speak a word of truth is the most important part of pushing through resentment or disappointment. Otherwise, we are just ranting and raving while feeding areas of hurt rather than having these areas healed. I am constantly amazed at God's ability to say even a simple sentence that He knows my heart needs to hear. It sets me free.

As I've written this book and led "Unforgettable" and "Stiletto Project" conferences the past two years, it has been during my own times in the valley. These truths have not come from the mountain top; they have oftentimes come from the foxhole.

God has continued to teach me how to walk through this tremendous trial as His daughter and His princess. I've also accepted that even though many areas in my life I would *not* have chosen to be part of my destiny, God's plans for me are *His* plan, not mine. I've had to take some of the expectations and put them in my "Moses basket" and release those to the Lord.

Before my experience in the airport that I shared earlier, I had no idea what it meant to fully behave as a daughter of God. The following principles have

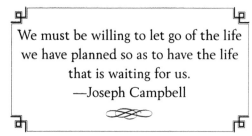

We must be willing to let go of the life we have planned so as to have the life that is waiting for us.
—Joseph Campbell

transformed my life as I continue to learn to grow in my relationship with Christ.

Be Still and Know that I Am God

Psalm 46:10 (NIV) says, "Be still, and know that I am God; I will be exalted among the nations, I will be exalted in the earth." This verse's truth has probably kept my sanity for a number of reasons—"being still" and waiting on God rather than running ahead and allowing my heart to fear has kept my focus on God's Word rather than circumstances. This truth has revolutionized my natural response system from a fix-it-myself mentality into "God will fix this" reality.

Behaving like a daughter means that I believe His word and His faithfulness more than I am impressed by the swirling storm around me. This has probably been the hardest truth for me to really embrace, and still there are times when I struggle to simply "be still" and trust God.

My outdoorsy husband George lived on a 48-foot vintage sailboat during his bachelor years. At the time, we both lived in New Orleans, Louisiana, where hurricanes were a common part of summertime adventure. Being a native of New Orleans, I was all too familiar with hurricane season, evacuations, and flooding that would threaten the city.

George and I had been dating for a while when one of the summertime hurricanes was approaching New Orleans. James and I were preparing to evacuate during the storm, as was most of the city of New Orleans. To my surprise, George was not going to evacuate; he was going to remain on his sailboat during the storm (yes, you read this correctly). Quite honestly, the thought of remaining in New Orleans during a hurricane had never crossed my mind. I thought remaining in a sailboat on the water during a hurricane was a little crazy. However, George apparently had ridden out many hurricanes during his rugged bachelor years on his sailboat. I wasn't sure where James and I would evacuate and was trying to figure our destination plans, when George called and asked, "Steph, why don't you and James stay on the sailboat with me while the hurricane comes through? It really is quite safe, and the hurricane appears to be a mild one. It will be a great adventure!" Although I thought this invitation was probably the wildest one I had ever received, my sense of adventure was kind of excited for the challenge! (The sailboat would be secured in the marina slip, so it was not like being in the open seas.) I asked James what he thought about the idea, and he was up for the challenge as well, so we agreed to stay on the sailboat during the storm with George.

While a good part of the population was leaving the city for the hurricane's arrival, James, George, and I purchased groceries, batteries, and supplies to spend the day in the marina on the sailboat. I called my parents to tell them where James and I would be "evacuating." My father, who is a marine engineer and has built many ships in his lifetime, knew that we would be fine and thought it would be a great adventure. Mom, who has never been on a sailboat, or, for that matter does not even like to swim, thought surely I had lost my mind. Dad reassured her that we would be fine. Dad was excited for us, and Mom, I am sure, spent the night praying for our safety.

The winds and water began to rise as the storm blew in. George, the professional sailor that he is, began walking around the boat to adjust the lines (ropes) to allow for the rising water. He took James with him and taught him the importance of paying attention to the lines while the storm continued moving in. We made a large pot of coffee and shared stories together while the hurricane moved closer inland. Our adventure was beginning, and we stayed up all night to continue to adjust the boat's lines during the storm.

As I sat on the deck of the boat enjoying the cool breeze (which is rare in New Orleans summertime), I watched George and James adjusting the lines over and again. They also walked up and down the marina dock to check on the neighboring boats to make sure their lines were secure as well.

The storm finally arrived and had winds up to 120 miles an hour with accompanying rain and rising water. Before long, we couldn't see the dock, and James and George continued to adjust the boat to the storm. I continued to prepare snacks and make coffee for the crew for our all-night vigil. As the sun began to rise in the morning, the rain stopped and the storm passed. I felt a real sense of excitement over this adventure that I originally thought was a little crazy.

George taught James, who was fourteen, how to weather a storm. God taught me how to be still and trust, even if I did not understand. I can easily look back and realize the

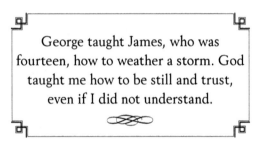

George taught James, who was fourteen, how to weather a storm. God taught me how to be still and trust, even if I did not understand.

powerful lessons God was teaching then that for which we have been thankful.

No Weapon Formed against Me Will Prosper ...

Isaiah 54:17 (AMP) has an important message. This verse says, "But no weapon that is formed against you shall prosper, and every tongue that shall rise against you in judgment you shall show to be in the wrong. This [peace, righteousness, security, triumph over opposition] is the heritage of the servants of the Lord [those in whom the ideal Servant of the Lord is reproduced]; this is the righteousness or the vindication which they obtain from Me [this is that which I impart to them as their justification], says the Lord."

This verse tells me that God has my back. The enemy, Satan, seeks to destroy me and rob my peace and joy and cause me to fear. The enemy also wants to convince God's daughters that God is an absent Father who is okay with bad things happening in our lives. This is a lie and contradicts the very nature of God's heart.

Satan's weapons can come in many forms. Fear, anxiety, doubt, disappointment, unworthiness, and low self-esteem, are a just a few of the ways that Satan tries to keep us defeated and convince us that God does not truly love us. We have all experienced times where we believed the lies of the enemy rather than trust the heart of God.

God has taught me how to more readily recognize Satan's weapons and stand in my position as a protected, loved daughter of God. Not to say I do not fall for the enemy's lies from time to time, because I do. The power comes from the core belief in knowing for sure that God will protect me.

As a victim of sexual abuse, I have had a difficult time embracing this truth. I realize as I write this manuscript that many women have had people in their lives recklessly rob their innocence. This violation makes embracing God's protection over us more difficult to work through, *but not impossible.*

During the season God was healing my heart from abuse, I asked God the hard questions. "Why did you let this happen to me? Why didn't you protect me?" These questions are natural to ask about horrific memories. What I've come to understand through years of healing is that we simply will never completely understand some circumstances here on earth. Secondly, because we live in a sin-filled world and people make destructive choices outside of God's will, they have consequences to their sin. Sadly, victims also bear the consequences of other people's sin. Even though I was the victim of another person's sin who chose outside of the will of God to harm me, God's grace to heal me has been so much larger than the abuse. We will have complete understanding of these situations only when we are in the presence of God. Until then, we patiently can rest in his grace and healing in our lives and know that God will right the wrong in the lives of the abusers. The weapon of abuse will not prosper in my life when I choose to live in grace and freedom rather than resentment and bitterness.

If God Is for Me, Who Can Be Against Me?

Romans 8:31b–32 (NIV) says, "If God is for us, who can be against us? He who did not spare his own Son, but gave him up for us all—how will he not also, along with him, graciously give us all things?" This verse exemplifies the heart of our Father who remains on our side and withholds nothing from us. We have it all.

I have wondered many times in my life if God is really *for* me. In fact, the difficulty I've faced in my life has made embracing the truth in the God's Word a little harder at times.

I recently was having a particularly hard day, and I felt like I was in the pit and really wasn't sure why. I was cleaning my kitchen, and my heart was filled with despair. I began to pray and ask God to take away the feelings I was experiencing. I tried to keep myself busy, hoping the feelings would leave. Nothing seemed to help. After several minutes I said to God, "Father, I know that you love me, but the storm raging around me is drowning out your voice. Please help me." I was quiet for several minutes. The Lord then spoke to my heart and said, "Stephanie, all of creation is shouting my love for you. Be still and listen." I began to weep as I quietly heard over and again, "I am for you. I see you. I have not forgotten you. You are mine." I began to pray out loud and thank the Lord for his faithfulness and love for me. As I did so, the despair and depression I was feeling left and the joy of the Lord returned.

Shortly after this experience, I heard this song, "You Are for Me" by Kari Jobe, which has become one of my favorite worship songs. I love Kari's voice and her music. Her music writing style easily identifies that she operates her life as a daughter of God. This song, "You Are for Me" expresses the beautiful Father-daughter covenant that He, indeed, is for us.

I know that you are for me I know that you are for me.
I know that you will never, forsake me in my weakness.
I know that you have come now
Even if to write upon my heart to remind me who you are.

125

God is for you and me. It's that simple. We are not alone. God is with us no matter what and ready to "graciously give us all things." He is prepared to equip us for everything we need whether it's peace, protection, provision, or anything else on the list of our needs. Matthew 6:7–13 (MSG) says

> The world is full of so-called prayer warriors who are prayer-ignorant. They're full of formulas and programs and advice, peddling techniques for getting what you want from God. Don't fall for that nonsense. This is your Father you are dealing with, and he knows better than you what you need. With a God like this loving you, you can pray very simply. Like this:
>
> Our Father in heaven, Reveal who you are. Set the world right; Do what's best—as above, so below. Keep us alive with three square meals. Keep us forgiven with you and forgiving others. Keep us safe from ourselves and the Devil. You're in charge! You can do anything you want! You're ablaze in beauty! Yes. Yes. Yes.

As this Scripture says, God has equipped us and provided everything we need, in advance. He is intentional in providing everything we need in order to succeed. At times when I have felt ill-equipped, this truth refocuses the heart of God toward me, His daughter.

God Is Intimately Acquainted with All My Ways

God knows you. He knows what you think and how you feel, and He knows even the deepest secrets in your heart. He knows you inside and out and eternally loves you. This truth is so important in order to behave like a daughter. It allows the freedom to be honest and real with God. It builds intimacy in your prayer time because you realize that truly nothing is hidden from Him.

You may picture God as a white-haired older man who spends His day seated on the throne, sending out orders to the multitude of angels. You may think, "Of course, God is concerned with famine, floods, and disaster, but how involved is He with the day-to-day needs in my heart?" This misperception of the heart of God is largely why many women choose to behave as slaves rather than daughters.

It's almost like we are doing spiritual acrobats in order to somehow impress our heavenly Father, when actually we have his attention 24/7. Psalm 139, which David beautifully

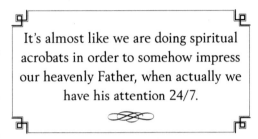

It's almost like we are doing spiritual acrobats in order to somehow impress our heavenly Father, when actually we have his attention 24/7.

wrote, is one of the many texts that describe the level of intimacy in which the Father possesses.

Psalm 139 (MSG) reads

> God, investigate my life; get all the facts firsthand. I'm an open book to you; even from a distance, you know what I'm thinking. You know when I leave and when I get back; I'm never out of your sight. You know everything I'm going to say before I start the first sentence. I look behind me and you're there, then up ahead and you're there, too—your reassuring presence, coming and going. This is too much, too wonderful—I can't take it all in! Is there any place I can go to avoid your Spirit? To be out of your sight? If I climb to the sky, you're there! If I go underground, you're there! If I flew on morning's wings to the far western horizon, You'd find me in a minute—you're already there waiting! Then I said to myself, "Oh, he even sees me in the dark! At night I'm immersed in the light!" It's a fact: darkness isn't dark to you; night and day, darkness and light, they're all the same to you. Oh yes, you shaped me first inside, then out; you formed me in my mother's womb. I thank you, High God—you're breathtaking! Body and soul, I am marvelously made! I worship in adoration—what a creation! You know me inside and out, you know every bone in my body; You

know exactly how I was made, bit by bit, how I was sculpted from nothing into something. Like an open book, you watched me grow from conception to birth; all the stages of my life were spread out before you, The days of my life all prepared before I'd even lived one day. Your thoughts—how rare, how beautiful! God, I'll never comprehend them! I couldn't even begin to count them—any more than I could count the sand of the sea. Oh, let me rise in the morning and live always with you! And please, God, do away with wickedness for good! And you murderers—out of here!—all the men and women who belittle you, God, infatuated with cheap god-imitations. See how I hate those who hate you, God, see how I loathe all this godless arrogance; I hate it with pure, unadulterated hatred. Your enemies are my enemies! Investigate my life, O God, find out everything about me; Cross-examine and test me, get a clear picture of what I'm about; See for yourself whether I've done anything wrong—then guide me on the road to eternal life."

We can agree that Psalm 139 outlines the heart of God much different than the stoic, throne-seated distant Father we may have pictured.

In my mind, I also picture God seated on His throne. After all, He is the king. However, I picture God sitting on the *edge* of his seat, with his chin securely placed in His hand while He watches over me, moment by moment. When trouble arrives, He sends help. When I am sad, He gives a word to encourage my heart. When I am simply being silly, He smiles and delights in me. He is *intimately* involved in my life—and in yours!

God's Covenant with Me …

Isaiah 49:15b–16a (NIV) reads, "I could never forget you, see I've carved you on the palm of my hand" and is the theme for which this book was inspired.

You are unforgettable to God. Erasing yourself from God's heart and mind is virtually impossible.

Through the amazing lives of the women we've studied together, we've been able to realize several attributes of *daughterhood*.

Hannah was relentless in her *prayer* time, petitioning God year after year for her child, Samuel. She repeats over and again in 1 Samuel, "do not forget me ... please remember me." I love the raw emotion Hannah displayed out of her Father-daughter relationship she had with God. She was tormented by Peninah (wife No. 2) and even accused of being drunk by the Priest, Eli. She persisted and waited. *God was faithful.*

Jochebed exhibited her *courage* in the way she carefully built an ark-like sailing vessel for her first born son. She willingly placed his basket in the river while she trusted God's plan. As a daughter, she followed through with this plan, even though it tested all of her natural responses, probably more than we will ever realize. The child whom she released was carried to safety and then miraculously returned to her. His adoption into the royal family prepared him to lead the children of Israel out of captivity and into freedom. *God was faithful.*

Elizabeth's and Mary's *favor* was realized through the amazing assignment God destined for these women. They made a choice to obey God and view them as being selected for a special assignment rather than an affliction. Their obedience fulfilled prophesies of the coming Messiah, which would eternally change the course of time. They chose to view themselves in the light of God's favor and sacrificially stepped into their destiny as vessels for God's amazing redemptive plan. *God was faithful.*

Mary Magdalene's *forgiveness* offered by Jesus saved her life and changed the course of her once sin-filled reputation. She chose to exchange the emptiness of her former life and embrace the peace-filled destiny God planned uniquely for her. Although her heart was broken with the death of Jesus, she remained faithful as she stood at the tomb and waited for the fulfillment of the word He promised. She was honored as the first person to see Jesus after his resurrection. She was chosen as the one who would proclaim the news that Jesus was alive. *God was faithful.*

These women—each unique in their individual way, but ordinary, like you and me—all have remarkable stories. One area they all have in common is that they chose to behave like daughters and not slaves and embrace the difficult, but fulfilling destiny God planned for them. They are indeed, His princesses, as are we.

God has an amazing plan for your life. It may not look like the life you originally imagined. But when it's from God, it will be so much greater than you could have ever dreamed. As you choose to embrace your relationship with God out of the Father-daughter heart rather than from a slave mentality, you will come to experience the grace of God, just like these powerful women.

My prayer is that you will be set free in order to embrace the most amazing, peace-filled, joy-filled life that God has to offer. It's yours. Christ's sacrifice paid for it on your behalf. *God is faithful!*

As Peter wrote in 1 Peter 2: 9–10 (MSG), "But you are the ones chosen by God, chosen for the high calling of priestly work, chosen to be a holy people, God's instruments to do his work and speak out for him, to tell others of the night-and-day difference he made for you—from nothing to something, from rejected to accepted."

Most of all, remember that in God's eyes, you are unforgettable. He is relentless in His pursuit of *you!*

10

HOW TO BECOME GOD'S DAUGHTER

HOW TO BECOME GOD'S
Daughter

$\mathcal{J}$f you are not sure of your relationship with Christ, this chapter will help you understand more fully God's plan for your adoption. This is a simple, but comprehensive outline of God's relentless desire to be in relationship with you.

Many times we equate our "goodness" with whether or not we are acceptable to God and whether or not we will eternally be placed in heaven or hell. Our eternal destiny resides within our free will to ask to be a daughter of God and inherit all the riches of the relationship with him. Heaven is our reward.

My son John Mark is the second born in our family. He has always had a more introverted and quiet temperament. His older sister, Jessica, and younger brother, James, often engaged themselves in activities that were loud and boisterous, and John Mark was often quietly building blocks or playing with toys. He loved to read and always liked to be the child that stayed out of trouble the most. He was the first to straighten up if he thought he would have disciplinary measures taken in response to his disobedience.

When was in kindergarten, the teacher asked the children to complete a survey that asked interesting questions about their likes and dislikes. This survey included describing a fun activity, sharing a favorite book or color, and describing one attribute about themselves that they really liked. We went to his kindergarten class on parent night and saw John Mark's survey proudly posted on the board. It listed his favorite foods, favorite pets, and most loved games to play. One interesting section was titled, "One attribute I like about myself." What was John Mark's response? "I like that I am always good!" We have enjoyed his perception 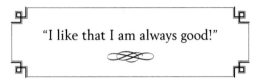 for many years and have fondly remembered his story.

"I like that I am always good!"

Your goodness does not even begin to measure the sacrifice that Christ paid on your behalf. The truth is that you cannot ever be "good" enough to equal what Jesus did for you. However, His grace covers what you cannot fill by providing a way to be adopted as His children.

You're not here by accident. God loves you. He wants you to have a relationship with Him through Jesus, His Son. Just one thing separates you from God. That one thing is sin.

The Bible describes sin in many ways. Most simply, sin is our failure to measure up to God's holiness and His righteous standards. We sin by things we do, choices we make, attitudes we show, and thoughts we entertain. We also sin when we fail to do right things. The Bible affirms our own experience—"there is none righteous, not even one." No matter how good we try to be, none of us does right things all the time.

People tend to divide themselves into groups—good people and bad people—but God says that every person who has ever lived is a sinner, and that *any* sin separates us from God. No matter how we might classify ourselves, we are *all* sinners. Romans 3:23 (NIV) shows what I mean: "For all have sinned and come short of the glory of God."

Many people are confused about the way to God. Some think they will be punished or rewarded according to how good they are.

Some think they should make things right in their lives before they try to come to God. Others find it hard to understand how Jesus could love them when other people don't seem to. But I have great news for you! God *does* love you! More than you can ever imagine. You can't do anything to make Him stop. Yes, our sins demand punishment—the punishment of death and separation from God, but, because of His great love, God sent His only Son Jesus to die for our sins. Romans 5:8 (NIV)reminds us of what Christ did for us. "God demonstrates His own love for us in this: While we were still sinners, Christ died for us."

For you to come to God, you have to get rid of your sin problem. But, in just your own strength, you can't do this! You can't make yourself right with God by being a better person. Only God can rescue you from your sins. He is willing to do so not because of anything you can offer Him, but just because He loves you! Titus 3:5 (NIV), "He saved us, not because of righteous things we had done, but because of His mercy."

God's grace allows you to come to Him, not your efforts to clean up your life or work your way to Heaven. You can't earn it. It's a free gift. Ephesians 2:8–9 (NIV)highlights that God's grace is what saves you. "For it is by grace you have been saved, through faith—and this not from yourselves, it is the gift of God—not by works, so that no one can boast."

For you to come to God, the penalty for your sin must be paid. God's gift to you is His son, Jesus, who paid the debt for you when He died on the cross. Romans 6:23 (NIV) says, "For the wages of sin is death, but the gift of God is eternal life in Jesus Christ our Lord."

Jesus paid the price for your sin and mine by giving His life on a cross at a place called Calvary, just outside the city walls of Jerusalem in ancient Israel. God brought Jesus back from the dead to provide the way for you to have a personal relationship with Him through Jesus. When you realize how deeply your sin grieves the heart of God and how desperately you need a Savior, you're ready to receive God's offer of salvation. To admit you are a sinner means turning away from your sin and selfishness and turning to follow Jesus. The Bible's word for this is "repentance"—to change your thinking about how grievous sin is so your thinking is in-line with God's.

All that's left for you to do is to accept the gift that Jesus is holding out for you right now, as Romans 10:9–10(NIV) says. "If you confess with your mouth, 'Jesus is Lord,' and believe in your heart that God raised him from the dead, you will be saved. For it is with your heart that you believe and are justified, and it is with your mouth that you confess and are saved."

God says that if you believe in His son, Jesus, you can live forever with Him in glory. John 3:16 (NIV) supports this amazing message: "For God so loved the world that He gave his one and only Son, that whoever believes in him shall not perish, but have eternal life."

Are you ready to accept the gift of eternal life that Jesus is offering you right now? Let's review what this commitment involves (say these statements to yourself):

I acknowledge I am a sinner in need of a Savior, which means I must repent and turn *away* from sin.

I believe in my heart that God raised Jesus from the dead, which means I must trust that Jesus paid the full penalty for my sins.

I confess Jesus as my Lord and my God, which means I must surrender control of my life to Jesus.

I receive Jesus as my Savior forever, which means I must accept that God has done *for* me and *in* me what He promised.

If it is your sincere desire to receive Jesus into your heart as your personal Lord and Savior, then talk to God from your heart with this suggested prayer:

> *Lord Jesus, I know that I am a sinner and do not deserve*
> *eternal life. But, I believe You died and rose from the*
> *grave to make me a new creation and to prepare me to*
> *dwell in your presence forever. Jesus, come into my life,*

take control of my life, forgive my sins, and save me. I am now placing my trust in You alone for my salvation, and I accept your free gift of eternal life. Amen.

If you have trusted Jesus as your Lord and Savior, please let me know. I want to rejoice in what God has done in your life and help you to grow spiritually.

11

THE DAUGHTER HANDBOOK

Unforgettable

The Daughter
Handbook

A daughter needs to know the word of God. In order to put all the tools in place to take the next steps in walking your journey as a daughter and living a life that is filled with God's purpose, you need to know the truth from God's Word. These truths also serve as a powerful weapon when the enemy tries to bring thoughts of doubt, fear, insecurity, or mistrust.

Neil Anderson, in his book *Who I Am in Christ*, has compiled a wonderful outline of Scriptures that I have personally utilized in my life and have used to encourage others. I keep these Scriptures close at hand as a reminder of *whose* I am.

I Am Accepted ...

- I am God's child.
- "Yet to all who received him, to those who believed in his name, he gave the right to become children of God" John 1:12 (NIV).
- As a disciple, I am a friend of Jesus Christ.
- "I no longer call you servants, because a servant does not know his master's business. Instead, I have called you

friends, for everything that I learned from my Father I have made known to you" John 15:15 (NIV).

- I have been justified.
- "Therefore, since we have been justified through faith, we have peace with God through our Lord Jesus Christ" Romans 5:1 (NIV).
- I am united with the Lord, and I am one with Him in spirit.
- "But he who unites himself with the Lord is one with him in spirit" 1 Corinthians 6:17 (NIV).
- I have been bought with a price, and I belong to God.
- "Do you not know that your body is a temple of the Holy Spirit, who is in you, whom you have received from God? You are not your own; you were bought at a price. Therefore honor God with your body" 1 Corinthians 6:19–20 (NIV).
- I am a member of Christ's body.
- "Now you are the body of Christ, and each one of you is a part of it" 1 Corinthians 12:27 (NIV).
- I have been chosen by God and adopted as His child.
- "Praise be to the God and Father of our Lord Jesus Christ, who has blessed us in the heavenly realms with every spiritual blessing in Christ. For he chose us in him before the creation of the world to be holy and blameless in his sight. In love he predestined us to be adopted as his sons through Jesus Christ, in accordance with his pleasure and will to the praise of his glorious grace, which he has freely given us in the One he loves. In him we have redemption through his blood, the forgiveness of sins, in accordance with the riches of God's grace that he lavished on us with all wisdom and understanding" Ephesians 1:3–8 (NIV).
- I have been redeemed and forgiven of all my sins.

- "For he has rescued us from the dominion of darkness and brought us into the kingdom of the Son he loves, in whom we have redemption, the forgiveness of sins" Colossians 1:13–14 (NIV).
- I am complete in Christ.
- "For in Christ all the fullness of the Deity lives in bodily form, and you have been given fullness in Christ, who is the head over every power and authority" Colossians 2:9–10 (NIV).
- I have direct access to the throne of grace through Jesus Christ.
- "Therefore, since we have a great high priest who has gone through the heavens, Jesus the Son of God, let us hold firmly to the faith we profess. For we do not have a high priest who is unable to sympathize with our weaknesses, but we have one who has been tempted in every way, just as we are yet was without sin. Let us then approach the throne of grace with confidence, so that we may receive mercy and find grace to help us in our time of need" Hebrews 4:14–16 (NIV).

I Am Secure ...

- I am free from condemnation.
- "Therefore, there is now no condemnation for those who are in Christ Jesus" Romans 8:1 (NIV).
- I am assured that God works for my good in all circumstances.
- "And we know that in all things God works for the good of those who love him, who have been called according to his purpose" Romans 8:28 (NIV).
- I am free from any condemnation brought against me, and I cannot be separated from the love of God.

- "What, then, shall we say in response to this? If God is for us, who can be against us? He who did not spare his own Son, but gave him up for us all how will he not also, along with him, graciously give us all things? Who will bring any charge against those whom God has chosen? It is God who justifies. Who is he that condemns? Christ Jesus, who died more than that, who was raised to life is at the right hand of God and is also interceding for us. Who shall separate us from the love of Christ? Shall trouble or hardship or persecution or famine or nakedness or danger or sword? As it is written: 'For your sake we face death all day long; we are considered as sheep to be slaughter.' No, in all these things we are more than conquerors through him who loved us. For I am convinced that neither death nor life, neither angels nor demons, neither the present nor the future, nor any powers, neither height nor depth, nor anything else in all creation, will be able to separate us from the love of God that is in Christ Jesus our Lord" Romans 8:31–39 (NIV).
- I have been established, anointed, and sealed by God.
- "Now it is God who makes both us and you stand firm in Christ. He anointed us, set his seal of ownership on us, and put his Spirit in our hearts as a deposit, guaranteeing what is to come" 2 Corinthians 1:21–22 (NIV).
- I am hidden with Christ in God.
- "Since, then, you have been raised with Christ, set your hearts on things above, where Christ is seated at the right hand of God. Set your minds on things above, not on earthly things. For you died, and your life is now hidden with Christ in God. 4When Christ, who is your life, appears, then you also will appear with him in glory" Colossians 3:1–4 (NIV).

- I am confident that God will complete the good work He started in me.
- "Being confident of this, that he who began a good work in you will carry it on to completion until the day of Christ Jesus" Philippians 1:6 (NIV).
- I am a citizen of heaven.
- "But our citizenship is in heaven. And we eagerly await a Savior from there, the Lord Jesus Christ" Philippians 3:20 (NIV).
- I have not been given a spirit of fear but of power, love and a sound mind.
- "For God did not give us a spirit of timidity, but a spirit of power, of love and of self-discipline" 2 Timothy 1:7 (NIV).
- I am born of God, and the evil one cannot touch me.
- "We know that anyone born of God does not continue to sin; the one who was born of God keeps him safe, and the evil one cannot harm him" 1 John 5:18 (NIV).

I Am Significant ...

- I am a branch of Jesus Christ, the true vine, and a channel of His life.
- "I am the vine; you are the branches. If a man remains in me and I in him, he will bear much fruit; apart from me you can do nothing" John 15:5 (NIV).
- I have been chosen and appointed to bear fruit.
- "You did not choose me, but I chose you and appointed you to go and bear fruit, fruit that will last. Then the Father will give you whatever you ask in my name" John 15:16 (NIV).
- I am God's temple.

- "Don't you know that you yourselves are God's temple and that God's Spirit lives in you" 1 Corinthians 3:16 (NIV)?
- I am a minister of reconciliation for God.
- "Therefore, if anyone is in Christ, he is a new creation; the old has gone, the new has come! All this is from God, who reconciled us to himself through Christ and gave us the ministry of reconciliation: that God was reconciling the world to himself in Christ, not counting men's sins against them. And he has committed to us the message of reconciliation. We are therefore Christ's ambassadors, as though God were making his appeal through us. We implore you on Christ's behalf: Be reconciled to God. God made him who had no sin to be sin for us, so that in him we might become the righteousness of God" 2 Corinthians 5:17–21 (NIV).
- I am seated with Jesus Christ in the heavenly realm.
- "And God raised us up with Christ and seated us with him in the heavenly realms in Christ Jesus" Ephesians 2:6 (NIV).
- I am God's workmanship.
- "For we are God's workmanship, created in Christ Jesus to do good works, which God prepared in advance for us to do" Ephesians 2:10 (NIV).
- I may approach God with freedom and confidence.
- "In him and through faith in him we may approach God with freedom and confidence" Ephesians 3:12 (NIV).
- I can do all things through Christ, who strengthens me.
- "I can do everything through him who gives me strength" Philippians 4:13 (NIV).

Who Am I in Christ?

- I am a child of God; God is spiritually my Father.
- "Because those who are led by the Spirit of God are sons of God. For you did not receive a spirit that makes you a slave again to fear, but you received the Spirit of sonship. And by him we cry, "Abba, Father" Romans 8:14–15 (NIV).
- "You are all sons of God through faith in Christ Jesus" Galatians 3:26 (NIV).
- "Yet to all who received him, to those who believed in his name, he gave the right to become children of God" John 1:12 (NIV).
- I am a new creation in Christ; old things have passed away and all things have become new.
- "Therefore, if anyone is in Christ, he is a new creation; the old has gone, the new has come" 2 Corinthians 5:17 (NIV).
- I am in Christ.
- "You are all sons of God through faith in Christ Jesus, for all of you who were baptized into Christ have clothed yourselves with Christ. There is neither Jew nor Greek, slave nor free, male nor female, for you are all one in Christ Jesus" Galatians 3:26, 28 (NIV).
- I am an heir with the Father and a joint heir with Christ.
- "Because you are sons, God sent the Spirit of his Son into our hearts, the Spirit who calls out, 'Abba,' so you are no longer a slave, but a son; and since you are a son, God has made you also an heir" Galatians 4:6–7.
- "Now if we are children, then we are heirs of God and co-heirs with Christ, if indeed we share in his sufferings in order that we may also share in his glory" Romans 8:17 (NIV).

- I am reconciled to God and am an ambassador of reconciliation for Him.
- "All this is from God, who reconciled us to himself through Christ and gave us the ministry of reconciliation: that God was reconciling the world to himself in Christ, not counting men's sins against them. And he has committed to us the message of reconciliation" 2 Corinthians 5:18–19 (NIV).
- I am a saint.
- "Paul, an apostle of Christ Jesus by the will of God, to the saints in Ephesus, the faithful in Christ Jesus" Ephesians 1:1 (NIV):
- "to the church of God in Corinth, to those sanctified in Christ Jesus and called to be holy, together with all those everywhere who call on the name of our Lord Jesus Christ their Lord and ours" 1 Corinthians 1:2 (NIV):
- "Paul and Timothy, servants of Christ Jesus, to all the saints in Christ Jesus at Philippi, together with the overseers and deacons" Philippians 1:1 (NIV):
- I am God's *work*manship, created in Christ for good works.
- "For we are God's workmanship, created in Christ Jesus to do good works, which God prepared in advance for us to do" Ephesians 2:10 (NIV).
- I am a citizen of heaven.
- "Consequently, you are no longer foreigners and aliens, but fellow citizens with God's people and members of God's household" (Ephesians 2:19).
- "But our citizenship is in heaven. And we eagerly await a Savior from there, the Lord Jesus Christ" Philippians 3:20 (NIV).
- I am a member of Christ's body.

- "Now you are the body of Christ, and each one of you is a part of it" 1 Corinthians 12:27 (NIV).
- I am united to the Lord and am one spirit with Him.
- "But he who unites himself with the Lord is one with him in spirit" 1 Corinthians 6:17 (NIV).
- I am the temple of the Holy Spirit.
- "Don't you know that you yourselves are God's temple and that God's Spirit lives in you" 1 Corinthians 3:16 (NIV)?
- "Do you not know that your body is a temple of the Holy Spirit, who is in you, whom you have received from God? You are not your own" 1 Corinthians6:19 (NIV).
- I am a friend of Christ.
- "I no longer call you servants, because a servant does not know his master's business. Instead, I have called you friends, for everything that I learned from my Father I have made known to you" John 15:15 (NIV).
- I am a slave of righteousness.
- "God made him who had no sin to be sin for us, so that in him we might become the righteousness of God" Romans 6:18 (NIV).
- I am the righteousness of God in Christ.
- "God made him who had no sin to be sin for us, so that in him we might become the righteousness of God" 2 Corinthians 5:21 (NIV).
- I am enslaved to God.
- "But now that you have been set free from sin and have become slaves to God, the benefit you reap leads to holiness, and the result is eternal life" Romans 6:22 (NIV).
- I am chosen and ordained by Christ to bear fruit.
- "You did not choose me, but I chose you and appointed you to go and bear fruit that will last. Then the Father

will give you whatever you ask in my name" John 15:16 (NIV).

- I am a prisoner of Christ.
- "For this reason I, Paul, the prisoner of Christ Jesus for the sake of you Gentiles" Ephesians 3:1 (NIV).
- "As a prisoner for the Lord, then, I urge you to live a life worthy of the calling you have received" Ephesians 4:1 (NIV).
- I am righteous and holy.
- "And to put on the new self, created to be like God in true righteousness and holiness" Ephesians 4:24 (NIV).
- I am hidden with Christ in God.
- "For you died, and your life is now hidden with Christ in God" Colossians 3:3 (NIV).
- I am the salt of the earth.
- "You are the salt of the earth. But if the salt loses its saltiness, how can it be made salty again? It is no longer good for anything, except to be thrown out and trampled by men" Matthew 5:13 (NIV).
- I am the light of the world.
- "You are the light of the world. A city on a hill cannot be hidden" Matthew 5:14 (NIV).
- I am part of the true vine.
- "I am the true vine, and my Father is the gardener. He cuts off every branch in me that bears no fruit, while every branch that does bear fruit he prunes so that it will be even more fruitful" John 15:1-2 I(NIV).
- I am filled with the divine nature of Christ and escape the corruption that is in the world through lust.
- "Through these he has given us his very great and precious promises, so that through them you may participate in the divine nature and escape the corruption in the world caused by evil desires" 2 Peter 1:4 (NIV).

- I am an expression of the life of Christ.
- "When Christ, who is your life, appears, then you also will appear with him in glory" Colossians 3:4 (NIV).
- I am chosen of God, holy and dearly loved.
- "Therefore, as God's chosen people, holy and dearly loved, clothe yourselves with compassion, kindness, humility, gentleness, and patience" Colossians 3:12 (NIV).
- "For we know, brothers loved by God, that he has chosen you" 1 Thessalonians 1:4 (NIV).
- I am a child of light.
- "You are all sons of the light and sons of the day. We do not belong to the night or to the darkness" 1 Thessalonians 5:5 (NIV).
- I am a partaker of a heavenly calling.
- "Therefore, holy brothers, who share in the heavenly calling, fix your thoughts on Jesus, the apostle and high priest whom we confess" Hebrews 3:1 (NIV).
- I am more than a conqueror though Christ.
- "No, in all these things we are more than conquerors through him who loved us" Romans 8:37.
- I am a partaker with Christ and share in His life.
- "We have come to share in Christ if we hold firmly till the end the confidence we had at first" Hebrews 3:14 (NIV).
- I am one of God's living stones, being built up in Christ as a spiritual house.
- "You also, like living stones, are being built into a spiritual house to be a holy priesthood offering spiritual sacrifices acceptable to God through Jesus Christ" 1 Peter 2:5 (NIV).
- I am a chosen generation, a royal priest hood, a holy nation.

- "But you are a chosen people, a royal priest hood, a holy nation, a people belonging to God, that you may declare the praises of him who called you out of darkness into his wonderful light" 1 Peter 2:9 (NIV).
- I am the devil's enemy.
- "Be self-controlled and alert. Your enemy the devil prowls around like a roaring lion looking for someone to devour" 1 Peter 5:8 (NIV).
- I am born again by the Spirit of God.
- "In reply Jesus declared, 'I tell you the truth, no one can see the kingdom of God unless he is born again.' 'How can a man be born when he is old?' Nicodemus asked. 'Surely he cannot enter a second time into his mother's womb to be born!' Jesus answered, 'I tell you the truth, no one can enter the kingdom of God unless he is born of water and the Spirit. Flesh gives birth to flesh, but the Spirit gives birth to spirit" John 3:3–6 (NIV).
- I am an alien and a stranger to this world.
- "Dear friends, I urge you, as aliens and strangers in the world, to abstain from sinful desires, which war against your soul" 1 Peter 2:11 (NIV).
- I am a child of God who always triumphs in Christ and releases His fragrance in every place.
- "But thanks be to God, who always leads us in triumphal procession in Christ and through us spreads everywhere the fragrance of the knowledge of him" 2 Corinthians 2:14 (NIV).
- I am seated in heavenly places in Christ.
- "And God raised us up with Christ and seated us with him in the heavenly realms in Christ Jesus" Ephesians 2:6 (NIV)
- I am saved by grace.

- "For it is by grace you have been saved, through faith and this not from yourselves, it is the gift of God" Ephesians 2:8 (NIV).
- I am a recipient of every spiritual blessing in the heavenly places in Christ.
- Ephesians 1–6 (The whole book)
- I am redeemed by the blood of the Lamb.
- "And they sang a new song: 'You are worthy to take the scroll and to open its seals, because you were slain, and with your blood you purchased men for God from every tribe and language and people and nation'" Revelation 5:9 (NIV).
- I am part of the Bride of Christ and am making myself ready of Him.
- "Let us rejoice and be glad and give him glory! For the wedding of the Lamb has come, and his bride has made herself ready" Revelation 19:7 (NIV).
- I am a true worshiper who worships the Father in spirit and in truth.
- "God is spirit, and his worshipers must worship in spirit and in truth" John 4:24 (NIV).

ABOUT STEPHANIE HENDERSON

Stephanie is a native of New Orleans, Louisiana, and the founder of Stephanie Henderson Ministries. With more than twenty years of ministry experience, Stephanie is well seasoned in biblical instruction, personal counseling, and the gift of bringing encouragement and hope into life's most difficult situations.

Stephanie's transparency and warmth provide a conference atmosphere where true ministry and personal connection are experienced. Through many difficult circumstances in her own life, Stephanie has decided to share a message of victory, not victimization, and speak life into the hearts of women.

Through grieving over the sudden death of her late husband and pastor, John Guerra, overcoming adolescent eating disorders, and breaking free from the bonds of sexual abuse, she has been gifted with grace to speak boldness and faith into many of life's darkest circumstances.

She shares, "When facing hardship, it can become difficult to believe that there is a better day ahead. So many times, I needed someone to walk through the circumstance with me and give assurance that I was going to make it. God did. Through understanding His Word and embracing His love, the Lord sustained, healed, and delivered me time and again. I am forever grateful."

Stephanie is a well respected conference speaker, counselor, and writer. She is happily married to husband George Henderson, and they reside in Colorado and attend New Life Church. They enjoy outdoor activities, traveling, and most of all, spending time with their family. Their family includes daughter, Jessica, and sons, John Mark and James. Moe, their five-pound Yorkie, is the family mascot.

Stephanie enjoys decorating, backpacking, rock climbing, event planning, and making fondant cakes.

Unforgettable -
God's Relentless Heart for His Daughters
- Study Guide and Workbook

Stephanie has written an exciting study guide for those seeking to "dig a little deeper" to further embrace the concepts shared in her powerful book.

This workbook expands the biblical applications of daughterhood and allows for greater insight through:

- **Personal Inventory** – How can I truly embrace daughterhood? Where do I need more faith? How can I successfully work through forgiveness? Who can be an "Elizabeth" for me?

What do I do with the "Penninah's" in my life? How do I really put the past in the past?

- **Scriptural Study** - A further enhancement of biblical truths and opportunity to experience transformation by knowing God's Word more deeply.
- **Prayer and Personal Journaling** - Journaling pages allow for authentic written dialogue with God and tracking steps of your personal story.

Stephanie's heart as a teacher and counselor is realized through the customized pages of this workbook. Through this study, she boldly challenges the struggles and victories of a woman's heart. This extension of "Unforgettable – God's Relentless Heart for His Daughters" is perfect for individualized study or small group participation.

For ordering details, please visit our website or contact our ministry through SHMinfoteam@gmail.com.

ABOUT STEPHANIE HENDERSON MINISTRIES

Our Ministry Exists …

to encourage women to experience an authentic relationship with Jesus Christ whereby they understand the Word of God, live out biblical principles, and embrace their personal destiny.

Through conferences, retreats, and gatherings, we are intentional in building relationships, sharing truth found in the Word of God, providing practical strategies for every-day life, and encouraging spiritual, physical, and emotional health.

We Believe …

that true fulfillment is found by having a personal relationship with Jesus Christ and understanding the truth of His word. We believe that the Bible is the only source or instruction for conducting life. Our conference formats are based solely upon the truth found in the Word of God.

What Conference Attendees Are Saying about Stephanie Henderson Ministries …

"The weekend, though short, was an incredible one! What a blessing you were as a speaker and friend to the ladies that attended the retreat. Your message was heartfelt, uplifting, and inspiring.

Many "jewels of truth and wisdom" were gained as you related our lives to debris and how through God and his love, we can see ourselves as he sees us, precious and beautiful! Thanks for touching my life and the lives of many who long to heal and grow."

Lisa

"I was at the retreat this weekend. I have probably been to fifteen women's retreats in my years of being a Christian, and I have to say you are the *best* speaker I have ever experienced! You are genuine and compassionate. Thank you for sharing your heart and thank you for speaking encouragement to my friend that lost her husband almost four months ago! Thank you for caring and sharing."

Lorie

"It was an absolute pleasure to listen to you and interact with you this weekend at the retreat. I had an amazing and revitalizing adventure—more than I ever expected. Your words rang so true for me. You are an amazing speaker, and I related to you in a way that was so much more personal and intimate than I ever have before in a conference setting. Thank you. Thank you for your words, your wisdom, your strength, your encouragement, and your heart for women and ministry."

Jennipher

Stephanie Henderson Ministries

Engaging, Equipping, and Empowering Women for Excellence!

Engaging

Our core value is to live, teach, and mentor through encouraging an authentic relationship with Jesus Christ. We believe that through this relationship and understanding God's Word, you can find all the answers to life's questions.

Stephanie believes that we need to have practical applications for putting biblical principles into place. Through sharing her areas of vulnerability, failure, and successes, she equips woman with encouragement for dealing with important life issues.

Equipping

Stephanie's ability to relate with women from various stages of life creates a relationship in which real connectivity is experienced. Through sharing topics both humorous and pointed, Stephanie is gifted in moving past the surface and truly relating to a woman's heart on a deeper level.

Being in touch with today's issues is an important key to women's ministry! Whether the needs are finances, family, or fashion, the ability to communicate clearly on important topics is vital to appropriately addressing the needs of a woman's heart.

Empowering

Our ministry believes that spirit, body, and mind are equally important in producing a healthy woman. We approach ministry from a stance of wholeness and victory—not imbalance or victimization.

Through biblical instruction, Stephanie brings a level of vulnerability and personal connection that allows women to feel comfortable yet challenged. The teaching is relational, the atmosphere is welcoming, and the result is life changing.

Endorsements

What Others Say about Stephanie Henderson Ministries ...

"I love the ministry that comes from the heart of Stephanie Henderson. Pam and I are so thankful for her wisdom, strength, and tremendous courage to boldly tell others about the Good News."

> Pastor Brady and Pam Boyd
> New Life Church
> Colorado Springs, Colorado

"Stephanie is a delightful woman who is always smiling! She has the joy of the Lord as her strength, and it shows all the time. Her love for our Lord is so evident that it comes out in loving other people around her, whether or not she knows them. A desire to help other women who have that same love for the Lord and grounding in His Word is in her heart. Stephanie's excitement about God is contagious. The courage she exhibits in trials is a testimony to women of all ages and situations in life. She wants other women to know that they also can be more than conquerors through our Lord, Jesus Christ."

> Tommye Hammel
> Developer of Training
> Precept Ministries, International

"I have been privileged to see firsthand how the Lord uses Stephanie and Stephanie Henderson Ministries both in the United States and internationally. She operates from the deep well of God's anointing. The anointing on Stephanie's life is very powerful and prophetic to break the yoke and set the captives free! Stephanie does not play games but draws on the anointing of the Holy Spirit to engage in true ministry to the deepest levels of a person's heart. She has paid the price of God's high call—this is visibly evidenced anytime Stephanie speaks, writes, or prays! I personally have been touched by the Holy Spirit's anointing on her life, and I have personally seen many others touched by it as well!"

Pastor Jeff and Jane Powell
Fellowship Church
High Springs, Florida

A Special Thanks!

Stacey Magnuson,
Picture You, Picture Me Photography

Thank you, Stacey for my photos! Your sweet personality made my photo shoot not only enjoyable, but relaxing.

Stacey Magnuson,
Picture You, Picture Me Photography

Stacey Magnuson began her career as a professional photographer on Bushiri Beach, Aruba, back in 2001. There she met her soon to be mentor, who in 2002 brought Stacey to Hengelo, Holland for a month of study. She soon discovered that people were her passion and capturing their hearts through their eyes became the goal of every photography session. It is the very essence of her photography. Stacey has had several of her works published and maintains wonderful friendships with renowned photographers, artists, and photographic critics across the globe.

http://staceymagnuson.zenfolio.com/

CPSIA information can be obtained at www.ICGtesting.com
Printed in the USA
LVOW08s0749070913

351413LV00005B/718/P